ALLIED WARSHIPS
VS
THE ATLANTIC WALL

Normandy 1944

STEVEN J. ZALOGA

OSPREY PUBLISHING
Bloomsbury Publishing Plc
Kemp House, Chawley Park, Cumnor Hill, Oxford OX2 9PH, UK
29 Earlsfort Terrace, Dublin 2, Ireland
1385 Broadway, 5th Floor, New York, NY 10018, USA
E-mail: info@ospreypublishing.com
www.ospreypublishing.com

OSPREY is a trademark of Osprey Publishing Ltd

First published in Great Britain in 2023

© Osprey Publishing Ltd, 2023

A catalogue record for this book is available from the British Library.

ISBN: PB 9781472854155; eBook 9781472854162;
ePDF 9781472854131; XML 9781472854148

23 24 25 26 27   10 9 8 7 6 5 4 3 2 1

Colour artworks by Adam Hook
Maps by Bounford.com
Index by Angela Hall
Typeset by PDQ Digital Media Solutions, Bungay, UK
Printed and bound in India by Replika Press Private Ltd.

Osprey Publishing supports the Woodland Trust, the UK's leading woodland
conservation charity.

Artist's note

Readers may care to note that the original paintings from which the colour
plates in this book were prepared are available for private sale. All reproduction
copyright whatsoever is retained by the publishers. All enquiries should be
addressed to:

Scorpio, 158 Mill Road, Hailsham, East Sussex BN27 2SH, UK
Email: scorpiopaintings@btinternet.com

The publishers regret that they can enter into no correspondence upon this
matter.

To find out more about our authors and books visit
www.ospreypublishing.com. Here you will find extracts, author interviews,
details of forthcoming events and the option to sign up for our newsletter.

Author's note

I would like to thank Jim Swan for the use of photos from his collection,
captioned here as Swan/Rudziak. Nicholas Rudziak was a young officer with
the headquarters of the First US Army who was part of a survey team that
inspected the Atlantikwall bunkers near Cherbourg in July 1944. In the
process, he took a unique series of photos. These photos would otherwise have
been lost had Jim not preserved them. Thanks also go to Mark Reardon, Ken
Estes for permission to use his photos of the Norwegian Atlantikwall gun
batteries, and to David Doyle for his help in locating several photos. Unless
otherwise noted, the remaining photos are from official US government
sources including the National Archives and Records Administration in
College Park, Maryland, and the US Army Heritage and Education Center in
Carlisle, Pennsylvania.

Glossary/acronyms

AA	Anti-aircraft
AOK	Armee Oberkommando: Army High Command; headquarters of a field army
AP	Armour piercing (projectile)
Baustärke	Construction standard thickness
CIC	Combat Information Centre
HC	High Capacity (US Navy high-explosive round)
HKAA	Heeres-Küsten-Artillerie-Abteilung: Army coastal artillery battalion
HKB	Heeres-Küsten-Batterie: Army coastal battery
LAC	Library and Archives Canada
MA	Marine-Artillerie
MKAA	Marine-Küsten-Artillerie-Abteilung: Navy coastal artillery battalion; sometimes shortened to MAA
MKB	Marine-Küsten-Batterie: Navy coastal battery
Regelbau	Construction design
SFCP	Shore Fire Control Party
SK	Sonderkonstruktion: special design
SK L	Schnellladekanone Länge: Fast-loading gun, (Bore) length
Tobruk	Small fortification with circular opening for crew-served weapon

A note on measure

Both imperial and metric measurements have been used in this book. A
conversion table is provided below:
1in. = 2.54cm
1ft = 0.3m
1yd = 0.9m
1 mile = 1.6km
1lb = 0.45kg
1 long ton = 1.02 metric tonnes

1mm = 0.039in.
1cm = 0.39in.
1m = 1.09yd
1km = 0.62 miles
1kg = 2.2lb
1 metric tonne = 0.98 long tons

Front cover (upper image): USS *Texas* firing her main guns. (Adam Hook)
Front cover (lower image): Batterie Hamburg firing. (Adam Hook)
Title page photograph: A projectile from Batterie Hamburg impacts behind
USS *Texas* during the 25 June engagement as viewed from USS *Arkansas*.

CONTENTS

INTRODUCTION

During the age of sail, the legendary Admiral Horatio Nelson quipped that 'A ship's a fool to fight a fort'. Was this adage still true in the age of industrial warfare in the 20th century? This book examines a World War II duel between Allied warships and the German Atlantikwall (Atlantic Wall). The central focus is on the German coastal guns of the Atlantikwall and the threat they posed to Allied amphibious operations. Who had the upper hand in such an encounter? As this book will reveal, Nelson's adage was not far from the truth, even in World War II.

The USS *Texas* has been preserved as a museum ship near the San Jacinto Battleground State Historic Site in La Porte on the north-east side of Houston, Texas. It was undergoing a major restoration at the time this book was written. (Library of Congress)

Amphibious landings were an essential element of Allied military strategy in World War II. The Royal Navy and the US Navy provided operational mobility that allowed the Allies to strike unexpectedly across the vast coastlines of the Mediterranean and Atlantic. Germany and its allies did not have enough naval power to seriously contest this, and so were forced to rely on other types of defences to counteract Allied naval power. The traditional approach was the fortified coastal gun battery. Hitler was enamoured of fortifications,

The M 272 casemates of Turm 2 and Turm 3 at Batterie Longues-sur-Mer. These were smaller than the casemates at Batterie Hamburg since they housed the much smaller 150mm TbtsK C/36 destroyer guns. These are some of the very few Atlantikwall gun bunkers with their original weapons still largely intact. (Author)

and his Atlantikwall programme became the largest and costliest fortification programme of the 20th century. By 1944, the Atlantikwall along the French coast contained about 1,950 coastal guns over 75mm in calibre.

Allied naval doctrine regarding the coastal gun threat evolved through time based on repeated experiences with enemy batteries during a succession of amphibious operations. The raid on Dieppe in August 1942 and the Operation *Torch* landings in North Africa in November 1942 revealed problems with Allied naval tactics when facing fortified gun batteries. The obscure Operation *Corkscrew* against the fortified Italian island of Pantelleria in May–June 1943 served as an experiment in determining the amount of force needed to overcome fortified coastal gun positions. When the Allies landed on Sicily in July 1943, they decided that the best solution was to avoid the most strongly defended areas of the coast. Nevertheless, the threat of Italian coastal batteries along the Strait of Messina deterred the Allies from attempting to stop the evacuation of German forces from Sicily, widely regarded as the only major blunder of the campaign.

By the time of Operation *Neptune* on D-Day 1944, the Allied navies had built up considerable experience in dealing with fortified gun batteries. There was a widespread appreciation that it was nearly impossible for warships to destroy fortified coastal gun batteries due to their small size, their excellent protection and the inherent inaccuracies of naval gunfire. This was especially the case if the Allied navies were limited in the amount of time assigned to the bombardment. However, the Allied navies also recognized that naval gunfire could neutralize enemy gun batteries for a long enough time to get the assault troops ashore. At that point, the invading force could deal with the gun batteries by capturing them. This proved to be the case on 6 June 1944 when the Allied navies successfully suppressed the German Atlantikwall gun batteries to the point where few if any warships were sunk.

The duel selected for this book examines the engagement between Batterie Hamburg, one of the strongest German gun batteries defending the port of Cherbourg, and an Allied naval bombardment group led by the battleship USS *Texas* on 25 June 1944.

CHRONOLOGY

1940
25 July   Batterie Hamburg established near Cherbourg.

1941
14 December   Hitler orders start of a new Westwall to defend Fortress Europe.

1942
27–28 February   Commandos capture German radar at Bruneval.
23 March   In response to Bruneval raid, Hitler orders Atlantikwall.
28 March   British Commandos attack dry dock at St Nazaire.
13 August   Hitler lays out expanded plan for Atlantikwall.
17 August   Dieppe raid underscores the threat of coastal guns.
8 November   USS *Texas* takes part in Operation *Torch* landings in French North Africa.

1943
January   Hitler orders Schartenstand Programm to reinforce Atlantikwall.
11 June   Operation *Corkscrew* on Pantelleria.
9 July   Operation *Husky* landing on Sicily.

1944
11 March   First air action against Batterie Hamburg.
6 June   USS *Texas* bombards Pointe-du-Hoc battery at start of Operation *Neptune*.
17 June   US VII Corps cuts off Cotentin peninsula.
20 June   18 P-47 fighter-bombers attack Batterie Hamburg.
21 June   VII Corps reaches Cherbourg Landfront defences.
24 June   Turm 3 of Batterie Hamburg knocked out during duel with US destroyers.
                 Initial bombardment of Cherbourg gun batteries planned but cancelled.
25 June   Bombardment Group 2 engages in duel with Batterie Hamburg.
26 June   US troops demand surrender of Batterie Hamburg.
27 June   Artillerie-Gruppe Montebourg agrees to surrender.
28 June   Batterie Hamburg surrenders.
15 August   USS *Texas* participates in Operation *Dragoon* in southern France.
25 August   HMS *Warspite* bombards German batteries near Brest.
1 November   Operation *Infatuate* landings at Walcheren island.

DESIGN AND DEVELOPMENT

ATLANTIKWALL

Coastal gun batteries played a pivotal, though often unrecognized, role in combating amphibious landings during the 20th century. Perhaps the best example of this was the part played by Turkish gun batteries in thwarting the Allied attempts to force the Dardanelles strait. On 18 March 1915, an Allied flotilla attempted to fight its way past the defences. The British and French navies lost three battleships, and suffered severe damage to three others from Ottoman mines and coastal guns. This was followed by the disastrous amphibious operation at Gallipoli. The Turkish batteries proved dangerous both for the ships at sea and the troops on the landing beaches. The failures of the Allied navies in this campaign would echo through the early years of World War II. Many Royal Navy commanders in the Mediterranean in 1942–43 had served in the Dardanelles campaign and remembered all too well the threat posed by coastal defences.

While Gallipoli represents one facet of the combat power of coastal guns, there was another lesser-known example. During World War I, the Kriegsmarine had emplaced coastal gun batteries along the coast of Flanders as part of the Marine-Korps Flandern. This eventually totalled about 225 coastal guns. More than half were powerful guns of over 6in. calibre with some as large as 15in. The role of these guns was twofold. On the one hand, the guns defended the German Navy's bases along the coast that were conducting U-boat operations against Britain. Secondly, the coastal guns deterred any

One of the sister batteries of Batterie Hamburg was MKB 4./517 Mestersand located in the far north of Norway near Kirkenes. The four 240mm SK L/40 guns were formerly with Batterie Skagerrak at Sylt on the North Sea, and were moved to Norway in 1941–42 at an early stage of the Atlantikwall programme. This shows a typical Bettungsschießgerüst in a kettle gun pit with an overhead camouflage umbrella similar in appearance to Batterie Hamburg prior to its 1944 reconstruction with gun casemates.

French and British attempt to turn the flank of the German land defences in Flanders by staging an amphibious landing on the coast. The only time these defences were seriously engaged was the Zeebrugge raid in April 1918 aimed at sealing off the U-boat base located there. The guns took a heavy toll on Royal Navy ships during the raid. The threat of an Allied amphibious landing on the Belgian coast never materialized, deterred by the coastal guns.

The Flanders batteries established many of the technical features of German coastal gun defences in World War II. The design of the bunkers, the layout of the batteries and the development of fire control techniques of the Atlantikwall were pioneered on the Flemish coast in 1915–18.

Following the defeat of France, Belgium and the Netherlands in 1940, the Kriegsmarine returned to the Channel coast. Kriegsmarine coastal guns located on the North Sea coast were moved to France and the Low Countries. These gun batteries were deployed around major ports, including Cherbourg.

Much of the German coastal artillery deployment in 1940–41 was offensive, intended to support the Operation *Sea Lion* invasion of Britain. The Wehrmacht installed a number of very powerful railroad guns and major gun batteries on the Pas-de-Calais. These began firing on Britain starting on 12 August 1940. These guns targeted British coastal convoys as well as ports such as Dover, Deal, Ramsgate, Folkestone, Hythe and St Margaret's at Cliffe. Britain responded with its own heavy guns that conducted retaliatory strikes against the German gun positions in France. Occasionally the German guns fired on Royal Navy ships in the Channel, but given the distances involved, hits were few. There were occasional successes. On D-Day, the Liberty ship SS *Sambut* was engaged by Batterie Todt and Batterie Lindemann, with two rounds striking the transport ship, causing it to sink about two miles south-east of South Sand Head, Goodwin Sands.

The focus of the German coastal batteries shifted from offence to defence in the summer of 1941 following the abandonment of the *Sea Lion* plans and the invasion of the Soviet Union. A British Commando raid against the Lofoten islands on the Norwegian coast in December 1941 prompted Hitler to demand the creation of a 'New Westwall' of defensive fortifications. Subsequent Commando raids at Bruneval and St Nazaire on the French coast led to further amplification of Hitler's original scheme in March 1942, that he now called the Atlantikwall.

Due to the heavy commitment of the Wehrmacht in the Soviet Union, the early Atlantikwall was modest in scope and seen as an economy-of-force option. Rather than deploying large numbers of troops, the Wehrmacht began deploying coastal artillery batteries along the Atlantic coast. These batteries usually consisted of obsolete German guns or war-booty French guns. An artillery battery could cover a swath of coast a dozen or more miles in either direction and so was much more economical than using infantry troops. German coastal defence doctrine assumed that the most likely Allied objective for any amphibious landing would be a major port, since the docks and other facilities would be needed to provide logistical support for the subsequent campaign inland. In the case of the French coast, German commanders assumed that the Pas-de-Calais would be the most likely site of a future Allied invasion since it represented the shortest distance between Britain and the Continent.

The ill-conceived Anglo-Canadian raid on Dieppe on 17 August 1942 seemed to confirm German defensive tactics. The raid apparently reaffirmed the Allied need for a port, while at the same time demonstrating that coastal gun batteries were highly effective in repelling Allied amphibious operations. The Dieppe raid further

The Pas-de-Calais region was the most heavily defended sector of the Atlantikwall on the French coast. This is Turm Cäsar, one of three S262 gun casemates of MKB Lindemann armed with the massive 406mm SK C/34 gun. It is seen here after its capture by Canadian troops in the summer of 1944. This battery near Sangatte, France, is now buried under the construction spoil of the Channel Tunnel. (LAC PA-133142)

The Kriegsmarine thought that the ultimate solution to coastal gun fortification was a rotating concrete turret for the gun. Only one of these was built as part of MKB Waldam near Fort Vert in France, based on a modified version of Regelbau M306. This photo montage shows it armed with a 150mm SK C/28 naval gun that was removed after the war. The battery Leitstand (fire control post) seen behind was a non-standard configuration. (Author)

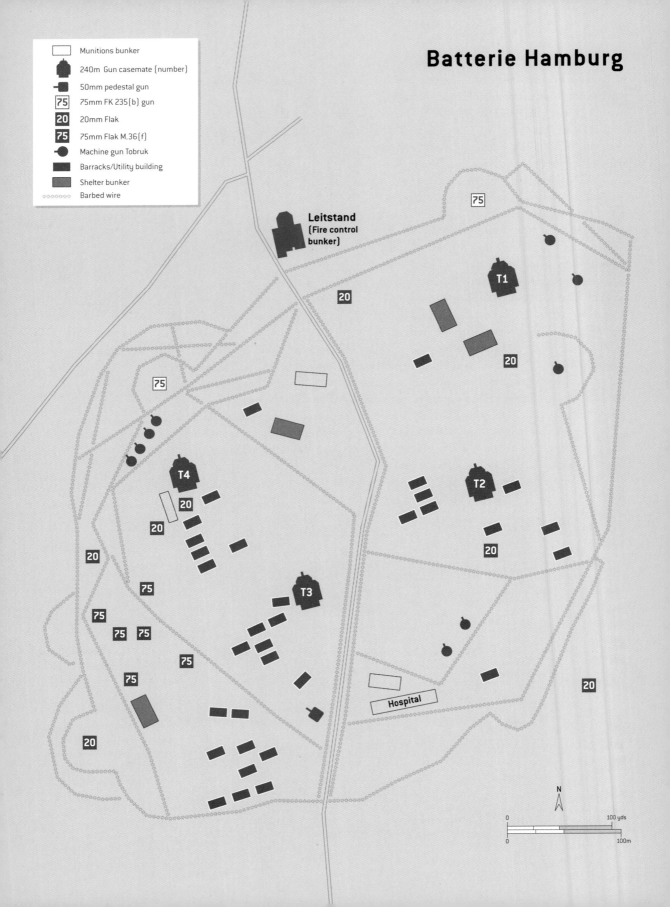

Batterie Hamburg

Legend:
- Munitions bunker
- 240m Gun casemate (number)
- 50mm pedestal gun
- 75 — 75mm FK 235(b) gun
- 20 — 20mm Flak
- 75 — 75mm Flak M.36(f)
- Machine gun Tobruk
- Barracks/Utility building
- Shelter bunker
- Barbed wire

Leitstand
(Fire control bunker)

T1
T2
T3
T4

Hospital

N

0   100 yds
0   100m

invigorated Hitler's Atlantikwall scheme, and led to a major increase in fortification work in late 1942 and early 1943.

Although previous German coastal defence efforts such as Marine-Korps Flandern in World War I had given the Kriegsmarine the primary role in such programmes, the Kriegsmarine did not have the resources in terms of manpower and weapons to match Hitler's Atlantikwall objectives. As a result, the Heer (army) gradually took the lead in the programme. Although there were no strict rules regarding defensive responsibilities, the Kriegsmarine generally took control of any defences in the immediate vicinity of ports while the Heer took responsibility for the areas in between major ports. As a result, both Marine-Küsten-Artillerie-Abteilungen (MKAA: Navy coastal artillery battalions) and Heeres-Küsten-Artillerie-Abteilungen (HKAA: Army coastal artillery battalions) were intermixed along the Atlantikwall.

The distribution of Atlantikwall coastal batteries was very uneven. In 1941–42, Norway received priority due to the numerous British Commando raids along the coast. By 1943, the construction of coastal gun batteries began to favour the French coast due to the increasing likelihood of an Allied invasion. Berlin continued to regard the Pas-de-Calais as the most likely landing area. As can be seen in the accompanying table, the 15.Armee (AOK.15) responsible for the Pas-de-Calais up to the Belgian coast had fewer guns deployed than 7.Armee in Normandy and Brittany. However, the coastline covered by 7.Armee was more than double that of 15.Armee, so the density of batteries was lower.

Atlantikwall Artillery by Sector and Calibre									
	Norway	Denmark	German Bight	Netherlands	France AOK.15	France AOK.7	France AOK.1	France AOK.19	Total
65–76mm	123	91	115	19	121	173	83	97	822
88–95mm	142	16	12	14	91	235	23	71	604
100–105mm	500	104	313	148	90	288	78	96	1,617
120–145mm	168	85	84	24	18	54	9	85	527
150–165mm	445	37	38	39	197	130	106	63	1,055
170–195mm	19	12	3	11	50	39	8	12	154
200–280mm	134	9	10	6	45	68	27	22	321
300–405mm	20	11	3	0	13	15	0	4	66
Total	1,551	365	578	261	625	1,002	334	450	5,166

Notes
This table lists Heer and Kriegsmarine gun batteries including dual-purpose Flak; it does not include divisional artillery.
AOK.15: Pas-de-Calais and Belgium.
AOK.7: Normandy and Brittany.
AOK.1: Bay of Biscay.
AOK.19: Mediterranean.

The types of guns used in the coastal gun batteries varied enormously. At the low end, some batteries used 75mm field guns. These were adequate for short-range defence of ports against small craft and minor warships. The most common were versions of the war-booty French 75mm guns. Some were the classic M1897 field gun, but many were the specialized variants including coastal guns on pedestal mounts, and anti-aircraft (AA) guns on high-elevation mounts. The medium gun category included many dual-purpose guns that could be used both in the anti-aircraft and anti-ship role. The most common gun calibre was the 105mm, and of these, the German SK C/32 naval gun was the single most frequent type. In the heavier categories, French 155mm guns and howitzers were the most common types, but German naval guns were also used. The most powerful guns in the 200–405mm range tended to be guns repurposed from naval mounts. Sometimes these included cruiser and battleship turrets.

Besides the dedicated coastal gun batteries, German army divisions sometimes had their artillery regiments deployed along the coast. These were intended primarily to fire against the beaches rather than against enemy ships and these guns are not included in the totals in the table. In addition to divisional field artillery, German static infantry divisions along the coast were issued a supplementary arsenal of guns placed in defensive fortifications along the coast. The most common of these was the 50mm pedestal gun. These were converted from surplus PzKpfw III tank guns and were intended to target smaller landing craft.

The Atlantikwall used standardized bunker designs designated as Regelbau (construction design). The specialized naval bunkers were designed by OKM-PiWA (Oberkommando der Marine Amtsgruppe Pioniere und Festungen: Naval High Command Office Detachment for Engineers and Fortifications). Bunker designs were usually based on several protection standards called Baustärke. The most common was Standard B with walls and roof that were constructed of 2m-thick steel-reinforced concrete. This was considered to be adequate to protect against the projectiles of

BATTERIE HAMBURG GESCHÜTZSCHARTENSTAND FÜR 240MM SK L/40-SONDERKONSTRUKTION

Technical data		Projectiles:	24cm Pzgr. L/2.6 (armour piercing)
Type	240mm SK L/40		24cm Spgr. L/4.1 Bdz (HE with base
Mounting	Bettungsschießgerüst		fuse)
Manufacturer	Krupp AG, Essen		24cm Spgr. L/4.2 Bdz u. Kz (m.Hb)
Calibre	238mm		(HE with base and nose fuse)
Length	L/40.13cal		24cm Spgr. L/4.2 Bdz u. Kz (m.Hb)
Tube length	9.55m		umg (HE with base and nose fuse,
Rifled length	7.82m		modified)
Weight	45,300kg	Casemate type	SK (Sonderkonstruktion: special
Elevation	-5 to +45 degrees		design)
Initial muzzle velocity	810–835m/s	Casemate height	6.5m
Rate of fire	1 round in 3 minutes	Casemate length	20m
Max range	26.7km	Casemate width	14.8m
Projectile weight	148kg	Construction material	6,720 tonnes (2,800m³) concrete;
HE burster charge	3.05kg (AP round)		23 tonnes steel
Propellant	42.8kg RP C/00 or C/06	Ammunition stowage	1,340 rounds (240mm)

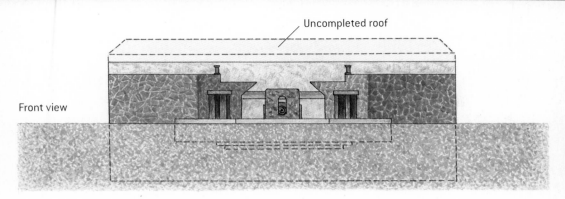

Uncompleted roof

Front view

Steel roof beam

Munition stowage annexe

Profile view

6.5m

20m

Plan view

14.8m

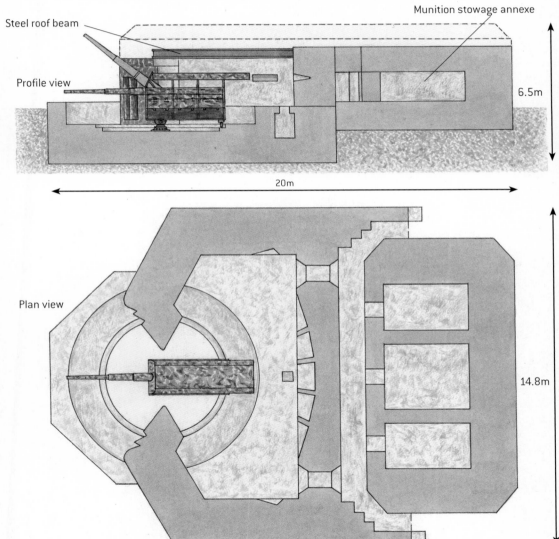

13

One of the largest guns deployed by the Kriegsmarine was the 406mm SK C/34 'Adolfkanone' intended for the never-completed H-class battleships. Unlike its sister gun at Sangatte in France, it did not receive a concrete casemate. Seven of these guns were deployed to Norway, including Turm Theo at Trondenes Fort near Harstad, Norway, with 5./MAA.511. This battery remained in service with Norwegian forces until 1964. (Ken Estes)

warship guns up to 210mm and 500kg aircraft bombs. High-priority structures such as the U-boat bunkers used Standard A that was 3m thick.

One of the major changes in construction practices took place in January 1943 when Hitler ordered that major Atlantikwall coastal gun batteries should be enclosed with overhead concrete roofs to protect against air attack instead of the existing kettle gun pits. This type of bunker was called a Geschützschartenstand, so this construction effort was nicknamed the Schartenstand Programm.

There was significant controversy about the Schartenstand Programm among fortification engineers in Berlin. Many of the engineers felt that the kettle gun pits were a better option. They argued that there was very little likelihood that a gun battery would be knocked out short of an unlikely direct hit on the gun. The gun pits also provided a much smaller target to naval gunfire than a large bunker since they were flush to the ground. Although the gun casemates did offer more overhead protection, their most important drawback was that they limited the traverse of the gun. While a gun in a kettle gun pit had full 360-degree traverse, guns in the enclosed casemates were usually limited to an arc of 120 degrees due to the limited size of their embrasures. In the event, Hitler's orders were followed, and the Schartenstand Programm gradually took effect in late 1943 and early 1944.

The Kriegsmarine was not entirely happy with the Schartenstand Programm, and proposed a more radical solution: mounting their guns in traversable concrete turrets. While this may seem far-fetched, new concrete casting technologies that used stressed wire instead of steel rebar offered the hope of lighter structures. A prototype of this type of turreted gun casemate was completed for Batterie Waldam at Fort Vert north-east of Calais. The resulting concrete turret weighed about 750 tonnes and was mounted on the turret race of the French battleship *Provence*. Battleship turrets of the time were in the 500–700-tonne range, so a traversable concrete turret was not as

bizarre as it might seem. In the event, only a single turret of this type was constructed. It would have been difficult for Germany to manufacture enough turret races for the many coastal gun batteries.

Another development in the Atlantikwall programme in late 1943 was the decision to treat each coastal gun battery as a strongpoint (Stützpunkt) capable of its own self-defence. This included both anti-aircraft defence and ground defences such as barbed wire perimeters, minefields and Tobruk machine-gun nests to repel paratrooper or Commando attack.

KRIEGSMARINE VS HEER

There were controversies between the Kriegsmarine and Heer over the configuration and weapons used for coastal defence batteries. The Kriegsmarine used naval guns for their coastal gun positions. This had several advantages including the availability

The Kriegsmarine re-used some battleship turrets including the C turret from the *Gneisenau* after the ship was severely damaged during an RAF bomber raid on Kiel. Armed with triple 280mm SK C/34 guns, the turret weighed about 800 tons. Turm Cäsar was re-assembled as the centrepiece of MKB Orlandet at the Austrått fort in Ørland, Norway, to defend the Trondheim fjord. (Ken Estes)

Batterie Longues-sur-Mer included an M 262 Leitstand on the cliff overlooking the beach. The upper level contained the battery command post including an optical rangefinder. Below it was a covered observation post, and underground was the battery's plotting room. A similar Leitstand was planned for Batterie Hamburg, but never completed. (Author)

of armour-piercing ammunition suitable for engagements against enemy warships. In addition, newer guns had onboard data displays that could be linked via cable to the main fire control post for prompt transmittal of targeting data. The Kriegsmarine preferred to deploy their coastal gun batteries as close to the coast as possible since their main role was engaging enemy ships rather than targets along the beach.

Kriegsmarine coastal batteries generally used a fire control post (Leitstand) that was patterned after warship practices, so there was generally a plotting room on the bottom level with one or more additional levels containing optical rangefinders and devices for measuring the bearing to a target. Naval coastal gun batteries tended to have more sophisticated fire control devices than their army counterparts.

Army coastal gun batteries tended to use ordinary field artillery. This meant that guns often did not have armour-piercing ammunition. While the guns were still effective against transport ships and lightly armoured ships such as destroyers, they were not as effective against armoured warships as the navy guns.

GERMAN COASTAL GUN FIRE CONTROL

The Kriegsmarine had two methods for fire control, called 'single point' and 'double point'. Single point fire direction centres were based on warship fire controls and required elaborate gun directors and other devices. Due to the expense of such systems as well as perennial German shortages, this type of fire control was largely limited to the largest and most powerful gun batteries. The more common two-point system was so named since it required two survey posts (Peilstand) located on either side of the

This is a Langbasis Gerät 42 H plotting board of the type used by German coastal batteries for determining firing solutions for its guns. Range and bearing data was manually inserted into the device which served as a simple ballistic computer.

battery's fire control bunker (Leitstand). The general rule of thumb was that each Peilstand had to be located about a third to a half the distance of the battery's maximum effective range. The separation of the survey posts allowed for more precise triangulation of the target. This configuration was also called the Long-Base (Langbasis) technique since the greater the separation of the survey posts, the more accurate the triangulation of the target. The bearing data was obtained by the use of a pelorus, sometimes called a telescopic azimuth indicator. It helped the survey team obtain precise bearing information about the target that could then be sent back to the main fire control post for targeting purposes.

The Leitstand fire control post was usually configured as a three-storey bunker. The top floor contained an observation post with an optical rangefinder. This determined the range to the target. Below this level was a covered observation deck, used for general observation tasks. At the base of the bunker was the plotting room and adjacent communication centre.

The key device used by each coastal gun survey site was a Peilsäule azimuth measuring device such as this one. Two survey posts located on either side of the gun battery were used to precisely triangulate the location of the naval target. This particular example is preserved at Trondenes museum in Norway. (Ken Estes)

During an engagement, the rangefinder at the top of the bunker fed data to the plotting room below via microphones incorporated into headsets worn by the crew. The plotting room at the bottom of the bunker contained a telephone exchange that received information from the survey posts and from the rangefinder crew on the observation deck above. Some bunkers also had connections to more elaborate sensor networks such as coastal radar stations that could provide early warning of the approach of enemy warships. The incoming data was provided by the communication crew to the officers in the neighbouring plotting room.

At the heart of the plotting room was a plotting table, often the Langbasis Gerät 42 H (Long-Base Device). This device included a map of the target area along with a plotting table with elementary calculating capabilities to provide a ballistic solution for aiming the battery's guns.

There were two basic techniques for data transfer between the fire control bunker and the gun bunkers. The most sophisticated naval batteries used automated data transfer that fed to the guns by means of data cables from the fire control bunker to displays on the guns themselves. This method was used with newer types of naval guns, and mimicked the same system used in contemporary Kriegsmarine warships. The gun crews used the data on the display to correct gun elevation and azimuth. Batteries using older guns, as well as nearly all army coastal gun batteries, used a field telephone connection.

ALLIED SHORE BOMBARDMENT

LESSONS FROM THE GREAT WAR

The Royal Navy had several notable experiences with coastal gun defences in World War I as mentioned previously, especially the Gallipoli campaign against the Ottoman empire, and fighting against the batteries of the Marine-Korps Flandern such as the Zeebrugge raid in 1918. These experiences led to both tactical and technical innovations.

One technical response was the construction of monitors, specifically designed for shore bombardment. These monitors usually carried a single turret with large-calibre guns in the 12in. to 14in. range, and were suitably armoured to resist enemy shore batteries. Royal Navy monitors were used in the Gallipoli campaign and off the Flanders coast. They were slow and unmanoeuvrable. The concept fell out of fashion after the war in favour of relying on more conventional warships. Nevertheless, a handful of Royal Navy monitors were used for shore bombardment in World War II.

The more important consequence of the World War I experience was the development of gunnery tactics to deal with shore batteries. Coastal batteries that were clearly visible along the shoreline could be engaged using normal gunnery practices. However, many coastal batteries were located some distance inland and were not in direct visual range of the warship.

The inherent inaccuracies of naval gunfire against small protected targets required some form of spotting for gunfire correction. The Royal Navy originally attempted to address this problem using a balloon tethered to a ship. This was a short-lived solution due to the vulnerability of the balloon. By 1915, radio-equipped aircraft of the Royal Navy Air Service had arrived that were a major step forward in engaging shore targets. The most common technique for conveying targeting information was for the observer pilot to use the clock method with north representing 12 o'clock. This provided the observer with a means to quickly identify the angle of the fall-of-shot relative to the target, while the distance could be estimated.

In the event that friendly ground forces were near the target, this provided a second means for spotting. At first, the ground spotters used optical devices to transmit corrections back to the warships such as acetylene signalling lamps. Tactical radios of the day were not robust or small enough for this task and suitable designs did not appear until the late 1930s.

The Royal Navy continued to work on these problems after the war. Important technological innovations in naval gunnery such as the advent of gyro-stabilization of

REGELBAU M 178 LEITSTAND (FIRE CONTROL BUNKER)

Technical data		Concrete required	2,100m³ of steel-reinforced
Rangefinder	Em-Stativ-Gerät bis 6m Basis		concrete
Observation devices	Richtfernrohr auf Zielsäule	Steel required	105 tonnes steel rebar, 5.3 tonnes
Plotting room device	L.S. Kleingerät C/30		construction steel

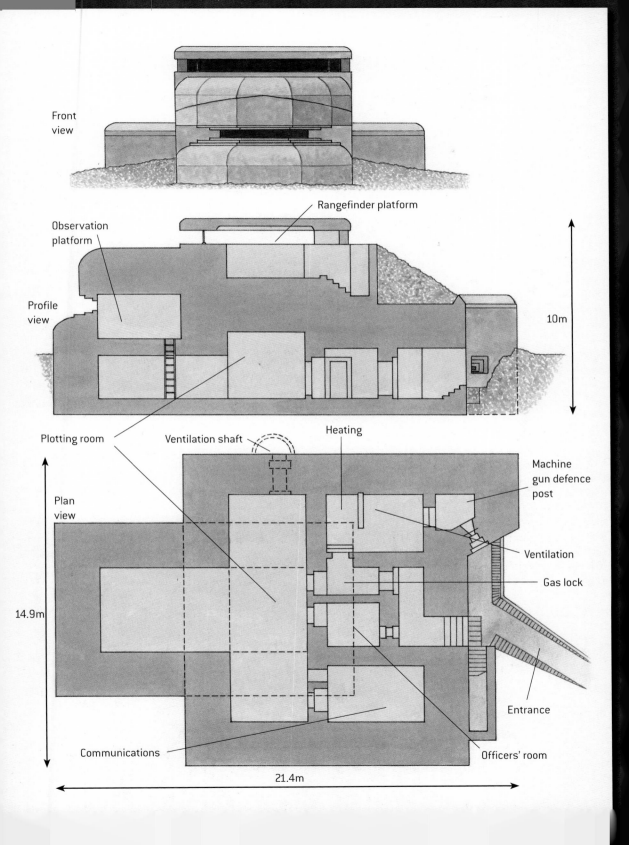

Front view

Observation platform

Profile view

Rangefinder platform

10m

Plotting room

Ventilation shaft

Heating

Machine gun defence post

Plan view

Ventilation

Gas lock

14.9m

Communications

Officers' room

Entrance

21.4m

Royal Navy doctrine regarding combat with coastal guns was strongly shaped by the costly encounters with Turkish forts on the entrance to the Dardanelles starting in November 1914. Here, British troops examine a Krupp 240mm L/35 coastal gun in Fort 1 at Ertuğrul above 'V' Beach on the Gallipoli peninsula. This gun was probably dismounted by a direct hit from HMS *Queen Elizabeth* on 25 February 1915.

fire controls helped improve gun accuracy. For amphibious operations, specialized spotting teams were organized; first called the Forward Observation Officer, and then Forward Observer Bombardment (FOB) parties. FOBs became the preferred method of spotting during amphibious operations since the teams had a better appreciation of the location of friendly forces, and so could reduce the problem of fratricide.

The US Navy did not have any comparable experience to the Royal Navy during its short participation in World War I. Nevertheless, there was considerable interchange between both navies during and after the war. The US Navy, and more particularly the US Marine Corps, paid special attention to the Gallipoli experience to provide guidance for naval gunfire support for future amphibious operations. Much of this research culminated in the US Navy's 1938 'Landing Operations Doctrine' publication that laid out the basic parameters of naval fire support.

Although US Navy doctrine strongly shaped US naval gunfire support practices in the Pacific campaigns of 1942–45, Allied practices in the Mediterranean campaigns of 1942–44 and the campaigns in France in 1944 were more strongly influenced by the Royal Navy. The US Navy's commitment to the Pacific dwarfed the deployments to Europe. Furthermore, Allied planning for the amphibious operations was dominated by the Royal Navy due to its greater experience and more substantial technical planning and intelligence resources.

EARLY LESSONS IN WORLD WAR II

The most shocking reminder of the threat posed by coastal guns occurred on 17 August 1942 during the Dieppe raid. The Royal Navy was well aware of the extensive

The Atlantikwall coastal gun batteries were strongly influenced by the experience of Marine-Korps Flandern on the Belgian coast in World War I. This is Batterie Friedrichsort/Göben, equipped with four turreted 170 mm SK L/40 guns from the old Braunschweig-class cruisers. Located in Zeebrugge, it took part in the defence against the Royal Navy raid in 1918. German troops demolished the guns prior to retreating.

German gun positions around Dieppe, but expected that a preliminary series of Commando actions would eliminate the main German batteries. Shore bombardment by the accompanying destroyers was restricted in large measure due to the probability of high civilian casualties in the neighbouring French towns. The Commando attack on the Hess Battery south-west of Dieppe succeeded, but the raid on the Goebbels Battery to the north-west was a costly failure. German guns sank or damaged every LCT (landing craft tank) involved in the raid, trapping the entire contingent of Canadian Churchill tanks on the beach.

The disaster at Dieppe reminded Allied planners of the risks involved in amphibious landings against well-defended ports. It was a major reason why the Operation *Overlord* planning rejected any landings along the heavily defended Pas-de-Calais coast in favour of the weakly defended Lower Normandy coast. Nevertheless, Allied landing capabilities in 1942 still required the capture of ports since there were very limited means to land heavy equipment such as tanks without docks and cranes.

OPERATION *TORCH*

The next major Allied amphibious landing, Operation *Torch* in French North Africa in November 1942, also focused on the capture of three key ports in Morocco and Algeria. Allied planners were well aware that the French Navy had deployed many coastal gun batteries near the target ports. Many of these batteries were old, having been built in the late 19th century; however, some were modern and had been installed in the early 1920s. The French forces in North Africa were still bitter about the Royal Navy's attack on Mers-el-Kebir on 3 July 1940. As a result, Operation *Torch* was a largely American operation so far as the land forces were concerned, in the hopes that the French were less likely to resist an American landing. However, the Royal Navy provided much of the invasion fleet.

Unlike Dieppe, the Allied flotillas had an ample number of larger warships to engage the French naval batteries if necessary. However, no large-scale preliminary bombardment was planned in the hopes that there would be little French resistance.

The US Army landings at Fedala to the east of Casablanca on 8 November 1942 were threatened by Batterie Pont-Blondin. This French naval battery was armed with two 138mm Mod 10 gun turrets taken from retired dreadnoughts. During a pre-dawn duel with the cruiser USS *Brooklyn* and the destroyer USS *Murphy*, the battery's ammunition, fire control centre and one gun were put out of action, but the USS *Murphy* was hit once. The battery was captured by Battalion Landing Team 2-30 in the early morning hours.

Instead, the initial objective of the landing forces was to seize the coastal gun batteries as quickly as possible, often using special operations forces such as Commandos and Rangers. The planning for Operation *Torch* included the latest techniques for shore bombardment including the use of spotter aircraft and US shore fire control parties (SFCP).

The Center Naval Task Force was assigned to capture the port of Oran in Algeria. US Army's 1st Rangers were assigned the capture of the Arzew batteries located to the east of the harbour. There was also a *coup de main* planned in Oran harbour, depositing US troops directly in the harbour from small Royal Navy vessels. The Ranger attack was successful, but the harbour attack, dubbed Operation *Reservist*, was a costly disaster when nearby French ships and anti-aircraft batteries sank the landing vessels. On the western side of Oran, Batterie du Santon began firing at several of the *Torch* landing sites in the pre-dawn hours. After daylight, it began to fire on two ocean liners that had been impressed into Royal Navy service as troop ships. The battleship HMS *Rodney* tried to silence the battery with its 14in. guns, but none of the projectiles hit the fortified guns. Even after repeated naval bombardment and air attacks, Batterie du Santon held out for more than two days, not surrendering until 10 November.

The landings of the East Naval Task Force at Algiers were also contested by French coastal batteries. The main threat, Batterie Lazaret, was targeted by a Commando attack. The French discovered the approaching Commandos before they reached the gun battery and were able to repel the British assault. The battery was attacked again during the course of the day, and subjected to repeated bombardments. It was finally overcome late in the day by a Commando assault reinforced by US Army self-propelled howitzers.

The seizure of Casablanca in Morocco by the West Naval Task Force had similar mixed results. Some of the initial landings had to be temporarily suspended due to the fire from French gun batteries. Eventually a combination of naval gunfire and direct attack by army units silenced the main batteries.

The lessons from Operation *Torch* were worrisome for Allied planners when contemplating a future assault on the Atlantikwall. The French gun batteries were not especially modern, and their fortifications were often antiquated 19th-century configurations. They were considerably inferior to the modern types of batteries being installed by the Germans in the Atlantikwall. The use of naval gunfire could not ensure the neutralization of hostile coastal guns, particularly so if the preparatory bombardment was curtailed by the need for secrecy, and concerns about civilian casualties. As at Dieppe, special forces attacks were sometimes successful against the coastal gun batteries, but these light forces could be repelled by a modest defence force if they lost the element of surprise. Clearly, improved tactics were needed before facing the Atlantikwall. On the other hand, the French batteries had never been able to completely halt the landings. They did delay and interrupt some of the landings, but in the end they fell to the combined-arms approach of landing forces supported by naval firepower.

OPERATION *CORKSCREW*: PANTELLERIA MAY–JUNE 1943

The next amphibious operation in the Mediterranean was also one of the most obscure: Operation *Corkscrew*. Pantelleria is a small rocky island located between Tunisia and Sicily. The Allies were preparing to assault Sicily in the summer of 1943. Pantelleria had German coastal radars that could spot an Allied fleet approaching Sicily, and airfields that could conduct raids on the invasion force.

Besides the obvious threat it posed, an attack on Pantelleria became an experiment to test the role of airpower in supporting amphibious operations. How much firepower was needed to ensure the neutralization or elimination of coastal guns? Beginning on 29 May 1943, Allied aircraft dropped 14,203 bombs totalling 4,119 tons on 16 of the 21 Italian coastal gun batteries. On 31 May 1943, a parallel campaign of naval bombardment began. The Italians continued to refuse Allied surrender demands so, on 11 June, the British 1st Division began amphibious landings near the main Pantelleria harbour. The shell-shocked Italian garrison surrendered with very little fighting.

With regard to the efficacy of the air attacks, a later US Army Air Force report noted:

> Despite the weight of the bombardment to which Pantelleria had been subjected, comparatively few of the coastal defense and anti-aircraft batteries were damaged sufficiently to prevent their being fired by determined crews … Scarcely more than 3.3 percent of the bombs dropped by B-17s fell within a 100-yard radius of the battery on

Troops of the British 1st Infantry Division come ashore on Pantelleria on 11 June 1943 during Operation *Corkscrew*. This is Batteria PT 382 near Punta della Croce, one of two fortified batteries defending Pantelleria harbour that were armed with the 76/40 Mod 1916 R.M. (Regia Marina) naval gun. There were 14 batteries with this type of dual-purpose gun on Pantelleria in 1943, used for both anti-aircraft and coastal defence. This particular battery was heavily damaged by the air bombardment of 23 May.

average. The corresponding figure for the medium bombers was approximately 6.4 percent and for the fighter-bombers about 2.6 percent. As a result of this lower accuracy, the bombing destroyed only about half the number of guns expected.

Even though very few of the gun batteries were actually destroyed, they were no longer combat-effective due to the collateral damage of near misses as explained in one report:

> Gun platforms were upheaved, electrical connections severed, and many guns that could have been called serviceable were so covered with debris that one or two hours would have been needed for clearance ... Because of the disrupted character of the terrain, the maintenance of an ammunition supply would have been a difficult matter, as merely walking from gun to gun required considerable effort ... Although the material damage to the guns was slight ... the bombing attacks had produced a profound effect psychologically. No battery was provided with adequate shelter for detachments of ammunition – a state of affairs that led the crews to abandon their positions and seek cover at various distances.

Operation *Corkscrew* convinced Allied planners that preliminary bomber attack was a critical supplement to naval gunfire in suppressing coastal gun batteries.

OPERATION *HUSKY*: SICILY JULY 1943

Operation *Husky* was the largest Allied amphibious operation until Operation *Neptune* in June 1944. The Italians had heavily fortified the island, especially around its major ports. The most important technical and tactical development displayed during the Sicily landings was the Allies' development of the means to conduct a landing away from a major port and to sustain the subsequent land campaign by moving supplies over beaches until a port was captured. This was made possible by the advent of significant numbers of new landing craft, especially the LCTs and LSTs that could land tanks and trucks directly ashore. Another innovation was the DUKW amphibious truck that could carry supplies ashore and immediately move them inland without the intermediate step of off-loading the supplies at the beachhead.

The implications for the coastal gun threat were dramatic. Coastal gun batteries, whether Vichy French, Italian or German, tended to be heavily concentrated around ports. If the Allies no longer needed ports to conduct amphibious landings, they could largely avoid the coastal gun threat by landing where there were few guns. This was welcome news for naval planners for another reason. In the Pacific theatre, Japanese fortified positions could be bombarded for days before an amphibious landing since surprise was

At the time of the Operation *Husky* landings on Sicily in July 1943, the coast was heavily defended by Italian coastal defence guns. This is an Ansaldo 152/45 S.1911, a World War I siege gun built under licence from the French Schneider company. These were deployed overlooking the Bay of Palermo area with two batteries of the army's 41° Gruppo d'artiglieria pesante.

not a critical aspect of the plan. In the Mediterranean and European theatres, surprise was a key element in all of the European landings. If the naval bombardment began days before the landings, the Germans would be alerted to the location of the landings and move their reserves to the beachhead. As a result, preliminary naval bombardment in the European theatre was inevitably brief.

Operation *Husky* conducted the landings at beaches that had few if any coastal gun batteries. As a result of the changing Allied tactics of amphibious warfare, Italian coastal guns played a minimal role in the actual Allied landings on Sicily.

Curiously enough, they had a profound effect on the final phase of the Sicily campaign. Sicily is separated from the Italian mainland by the Strait of Messina, only two miles wide at its narrowest point. As the defeat of the German and Italian forces on Sicily became inevitable by August 1943, Berlin ordered the evacuation of surviving units over the Strait of Messina so that they could fight another day on the Italian mainland. Due to the short distances involved, the evacuation used small barges, lighters and other coastal craft.

The strait was heavily defended by both Italian and German gun batteries. The defences included 58 Italian coastal gun batteries with over 150 guns on the Sicilian side of the strait, plus a further 66 anti-aircraft gun batteries and 153 20mm anti-aircraft guns. The Luftwaffe reinforced these defences with their own 88mm gun batteries bringing the total to about 500 anti-aircraft guns.

The commander of the Allied Expeditionary Forces, Admiral Andrew Cunningham, was all too well aware of the Royal Navy's debacle in the Dardanelles in 1915. He had commanded the destroyer HMS *Scorpion* in the 1915 campaign off the Turkish coast. The Royal Navy was well informed about the extent of Italian coastal artillery on both sides of the strait. The Allied navies were unwilling to risk their larger warships in the strait and believed that the air forces should silence the coastal gun batteries first. After the Pantelleria experience, the Allied air forces had little confidence that the numerous coastal artillery sites could be knocked out in the face of such intense flak. The coastal craft used in the evacuation were small and fleeting targets during their short half-hour transit across the strait. Neither the Allied navies or air forces were willing to endure heavy losses to stop the barge traffic, and, lacking firm instructions from higher authorities, attempts to halt the traffic were half-hearted. The Axis forces managed to evacuate 62,000 Italian and about 40,000 German troops across the strait, along with a good deal of their equipment. The failure of the Allies to stop this traffic, due in no small measure to the Italian coastal gun battery threat, allowed the Axis to significantly reinforce their defences in Italy.

The Sicily operation marked a milestone in the evolution of Allied shore bombardment. In combination with the lessons of Pantelleria, a new combined-arms doctrine was taking shape. At the operational level, the ability to land on weakly contested shores meant the coastal gun threat could be substantially reduced. The first draft plan for Operation *Overlord* emerged in July 1943 around the time of the Sicily landing. Instead of the landings being conducted near a major port such as Boulogne, Le Havre or Cherbourg, the landings would take place against weakly defended beaches in Lower Normandy. This substantially reduced the threat posed by the German coastal gun batteries of the Atlantikwall.

HMS *Abercrombie*, a Roberts-class monitor, seen firing its 15in. guns off Gela, Sicily, during Operation *Husky* in July 1943. *Abercrombie* was part of Task Force 85 supporting Patton's Seventh US Army and played a role in repulsing the German panzer counter-attacks of the beachhead. It subsequently served during Operation *Avalanche* off the coast of Salerno.

While neither air bombardment nor naval gunfire had proved effective in destroying a large fraction of coastal guns in previous operations, the bombardments were destructive enough to suppress the coastal guns long enough so that they did not prove to be a major hazard to the landings. But how much preparatory gunfire and bombardment was needed to accomplish this?

THE GRAHAM REPORT

In August 1943, the Joint Technical Warfare Committee of the British War Cabinet set up the Fire Support of Seaborne Landings Sub-committee 'to consider all existing means of providing fire support when landing forces on a heavily defended coast and to make recommendations, as a matter of urgency, for improving the degree of support'. The sub-committee was chaired by Air Vice-Marshal Ronald Graham, the Chief-of-Staff (Air) of the Combined Operations Headquarters. The resulting study was called the Graham Report.

Churchill's personal scientific adviser, Solly Zuckerman, had prepared a detailed report on the Pantelleria bombing campaign and the results of the Graham Committee were heavily influenced by its findings. Its report, released on 7 January 1944, concluded that naval gunfire might cause significant damage to German coastal gun batteries but would be more likely to temporarily neutralize the batteries rather than destroy them. Heavy aerial bombardment had a greater probability of destroying rather than neutralizing the batteries.

The report argued that the open kettle gun pits were vulnerable to air and naval bombardment, but the casemated guns were not. It was recognized that German gun casemates were impervious to typical 500lb/1,000lb bombs. Most naval guns except for 15in. battleship guns, could not penetrate their steel-reinforced concrete walls or roofs. Nevertheless, engagement of casemated guns could reduce their effectiveness due to secondary effects such as disruption of the battery communication, fire controls and ammunition supplies.

The Graham Report offered specific recommendations regarding the amount of firepower needed to achieve these results based on past experiences such as Operation *Corkscrew*. According to the report, a typical coastal gun battery in open pits could be successfully neutralized by a daytime visual bomber attack dropping 188 tons of bombs. Alternately, it could be temporarily neutralized by naval gunfire hitting the battery area for 10–15 minutes with a density of .05lb of 6in. naval projectile per square yard per minute; roughly one 6in. projectile per 2,000 square yards per minute. The aim was not to ensure the destruction of the German coastal gun battery, but rather to keep it suppressed long enough for the landing to occur without the gun threatening the destruction of landing forces. Once the assault force had landed, the gun batteries could be eliminated by direct attack from the land. The Graham Report formed the basis for the Operation *Neptune* Joint Fire Plan.

THE GREAT TEST: COASTAL GUN BATTERIES DURING OPERATION *NEPTUNE*

The selection of Lower Normandy as the location for the Operation *Neptune* landings was strongly influenced by its relatively weak defences compared to other areas such as the Pas-de-Calais. The density of Atlantikwall gun batteries varied from a high of about 4.1 guns per mile in the Dunkirk-Somme sector of the Pas-de-Calais to only about 0.7 guns per mile in Lower Normandy from Caen to Cherbourg, the future *Neptune* landing areas.

Not only was the density of German gun batteries lower, but two-thirds of the gun batteries in Lower Normandy were ordinary infantry artillery batteries, and not dedicated coastal gun batteries. Royal Navy intelligence reports typically referred to these as 'anti-ship' batteries since they were capable of engaging moving naval targets. The key difference between these two types was that the infantry artillery batteries

In contrast to Batterie Hamburg, Batterie Longues-sur-Mer was bombed during the Operation *Flashlamp* attacks by Allied bombers in preparation for the D-Day landings. This was the most sophisticated German naval battery near the Allied landing beaches, located between Omaha and Gold beaches. The four M 272 gun casemates are evident towards the top of the photo while the M 262 Leitstand can be seen closer to shore in the bottom centre.

typically lacked a Leitstand with a plotting room. The Allies were especially concerned about these anti-ship batteries since they could target the transport areas off the coast where the transport ships transferred troops into landing craft. This was the most vulnerable target during the amphibious operation, and a lucrative target for coastal guns.

These dedicated coastal batteries were under the direction of three army coastal gun battalions, HKAA.1261 with three batteries near Utah Beach, HKAA.1260 with four batteries stretching from Omaha Beach to Sword Beach, and HKAA.1255 east of the Orne River and Sword Beach.

Coast Artillery Defences Near D-Day Beaches 6 June 1944

Unit	Location	Weapons	Bombs (t)*
3./HKAA.1261	Saint-Marcouf	4 x 210mm K39/40	734
2./HKAA.1261	Azeville	4 x 105mm K331(f)	**
1./HKAA.1261	St-Martin-de-Varreville	4 x 122mm K390/2(r)	1,009
2./HKAA.1260	Pointe-du-Hoc	4 x 155mm K420(f)	1,183
4./HKAA.1260	Longues-sur-Mer	4 x 150mm TbtsK C/36	883
3./HKAA.1260	Mont Fleury	4 x 122mm K390/1(r)	775
1./HKAA.1260	Riva Bella	6 x 155mm K420(f)	886
3./HKAA.1255	Houlgate	6 x 155mm K420(f)	641

Notes

* Tons of bombs dropped on battery from April 1944 through D-Day. Tons = US short tons (2,000lb).

** Bombed along with adjacent Saint-Marcouf battery.

The *Neptune* Joint Fire Plan established the Allied tactics for dealing with the German coastal gun batteries. This was a multi-phase approach, starting with the bombardment

The only Atlantikwall battery that may have sunk an Allied warship was the 3./HKAA.1261 in Saint-Marcouf, sometimes called the Crisbecq battery. It was armed with four casemated Škoda 210mm K39/40 guns, two of which were in H 683 casemates like this one. On D-Day, the battery engaged the destroyer USS *Corry* off Utah Beach, but it remains unclear whether it was sunk by gunfire or naval mines.

of the most dangerous German batteries in April 1944 by tactical bombers of the US Ninth Air Force and the RAF's Second Tactical Air Force. Some of these initial raids were surprisingly effective. For example, the 25 April raid on the Pointe-du-Hoc battery by A-20 bombers destroyed one of its six guns, damaged two more and forced the removal of the guns from their kettle pits. These medium bomber attacks increased in intensity through May, severely damaging many battery sites.

The second phase of the attack on the coastal batteries was codenamed Operation *Flashlamp*. This attack, staged in the pre-dawn hours of D-Day by RAF heavy bombers of Bomber Command were designed to suppress the most dangerous gun batteries prior to the arrival of the Allied fleets. They focused on ten coastal batteries, with four singled out as posing a special hazard to the landing force: Pointe-du-Hoc, Houlgate, St-Martin-de-Varreville, and Ouistreham/Riva Bella. Over 900 Lancaster and Halifax bombers dropped more than 5,000 tonnes of bombs, Bomber Command's heaviest single mission to date. The tonnage directed at these sites is noted on the accompanying charts. In the case of some of these batteries, there was a follow-up attack by medium bombers prior to the arrival of the naval bombardment forces.

Bombing Attacks Against Primary *Neptune* Coastal Batteries				
Location	Battery	Tons to D-1	Tons D-Day	Total tons*
Pointe-du-Hoc	2./1260	487	696	1,183
St-Martin-de-Varreville	1./1261	398	611	1,009
Longues-sur-Mer	4./1260	176	707	883
Houlgate	3./1255	117	524	641
La Pernelle	10./1261	419	663	1,082
Merville	1./1716	917	380	1,297
Mont Fleury	3./1260	164	611	775
Fontenay-sur-Mer	3./1261	137	597	734
Maisy	8. and 9./1716	293	649	942
Ouistreham	4./1716	217	669	886

Note
* Tons = US short tons (2,000lb).

The third phase of the bombardment plan was the naval gunfire mission. These attacks were staged about 30 minutes before the arrival of Allied landing craft at nearby beaches. The intention of this bombardment was to prevent the reconstitution of the coastal gun batteries in the interval between the bomber attacks and the actual landings. Some of the casemated batteries received particularly heavy attacks. For example, Pointe-du-Hoc was hit with 250 rounds of 14in. naval gunfire from the USS *Texas*; Longues-sur-Mer by 150 rounds of cruiser fire. In the wake of these attacks, the Allied warships remained in the vicinity for 'on-call' gunfire support, directed either by spotter aircraft or SFCPs.

In the case of two batteries, Pointe-du-Hoc and Merville, there was a final special forces operation. This was intended to capture the coastal batteries to prevent any firing on the invasion force. In the case of Pointe-du-Hoc, this was accomplished by

HMS *Glasgow*, a Southampton-class light cruiser, served alongside the USS *Texas* on D-Day, providing fire support off Omaha Beach. During the operations of Bombardment Group 1 off Cherbourg on 25–26 June, *Glasgow* engaged in a duel with the 170mm SK L/40 coastal guns of Batterie Yorck near Amfreville and was damaged by two hits.

landing Rangers at the site from landing craft. In the case of the Merville battery, it was accomplished using a British airborne force landed by gliders.

While it might seem impossible that any of these coastal batteries survived the devastating *Flashlamp* raids, in fact several remained active. The most dangerous proved to be the Saint-Marcouf/Crisbecq batteries north-west of Utah Beach and the Longues-sur-Mer battery between Omaha and Gold beaches. These were the only coastal batteries that persistently fired on the Allied navies on D-Day.

The Saint-Marcouf coastal guns consisted of two neighbouring casemated batteries of HKAA.1261 – the 2.Batterie armed with 105mm K331(f) guns, and the 3.Batterie near Crisbecq armed with massive 210mm guns. On D-Day morning, they began firing at the US Navy destroyers USS *Corry* and *Fitch* around dawn. Both destroyers were supposed to be shielded by a smokescreen, but *Corry* came under fire as soon as it left the smokescreen. While trying to evade the fire, *Corry* struck a mine around 0633, cutting it in half. German accounts claim it was a victim of the Saint-Marcouf coastal guns but a later US Navy enquiry concluded it was a mine. The reason for *Corry*'s loss remains controversial. If it was in fact a victim of the German gun batteries, it was the only major warship lost to coastal guns on D-Day.

The two batteries were subjected to continual naval bombardment afterwards, starting with the cruiser USS *Quincy* and subsequently the battleship USS *Nevada*. The Crisbecq battery lost the first of three guns in the early morning exchange, the second at 1557 and the last at 1830. The batteries' numerous bunkers served as the cornerstone of the German defences north of Utah Beach and they were gradually reduced by US infantry attacks on 9–11 June. Oberleutnant zur See Walter Ohmsen, the Crisbecq commander, was awarded the Knight's Cross for his defence of the battery site.

Longues-sur-Mer, the 4.Batterie of HKAA.1260, was the only Kriegsmarine coastal artillery battery in the *Neptune* landing area. It included four casemated 150mm destroyer guns, but its full fire-control suite had not yet been installed. A destructive Operation *Flashlamp* raid tore up the communication cables between the Leitstand and gun casemates, impairing the accuracy of its guns. The cruiser HMS *Ajax* bombarded the battery starting at 0530 without inflicting any major damage. Around 0600, the German guns began firing on the command ship HMS *Bulolo*, forcing it to move station. HMS *Ajax* along with HMS *Argonaut* began bombarding the battery again, firing another 179 rounds. Two of the German guns were knocked out by direct hits through the open embrasures, and the battery ceased fire around 0845. The German gun crews cleared the debris in front of the two surviving gun embrasures by the late morning, and they began firing at ships towards the eastern side of Omaha Beach. The French cruiser *Georges Leygues*, assigned to defend Omaha Beach, silenced the two guns in the afternoon. During the course of D-Day, the Longues-sur-Mer battery fired 115 rounds against various Allied ships without scoring a single hit. The battery was finally captured late on the morning of 7 June by the 2nd Devons of the British 231 Brigade.

The heaviest engagements between the Allied navies and the Atlantikwall gun batteries occurred in late June 1944 around the heavily fortified port of Cherbourg. This is the focus of this book and is covered in detail below.

POST-*NEPTUNE* ENGAGEMENTS

The next phase of Operation *Overlord* was Operation *Dragoon*, the invasion of southern France. The Mediterranean extension of the Atlantikwall was sometimes called the Südwall. It extended along the French Mediterranean coastline down the Italian frontier to the ports of La Spezia and Genoa. The initial spine of the Südwall was formed from existing French and Italian fortifications and gun batteries, supplemented by new German construction based on the same Regelbau bunkers as the rest of the Atlantikwall. Of the planned 310km of coastal fortifications, only 87km were completed. There were 199 active coast defence batteries between Marseilles and Nice including 647 guns in the 75–340mm calibres. As was the case with Operation *Neptune*, the Allies selected a weakly defended portion of the Südwall for the *Dragoon* landings, along the Var/Riviera coastline rather than heavily defended ports such as Toulon and Marseilles. The invasion sector had 29 coast defence batteries with 88 guns, of which 34 were in casemates.

As in the case of the Normandy landings, the US and French landings on the Riviera coast were preceded by heavy air attacks and naval bombardment of the German gun batteries. The Südwall was largely ineffective in resisting the Allied landings. The only seriously contested landing site was Camel Beach in the Golfe de Fréjus on either side of the port of St Raphäel. The most heavily fortified portions of the Südwall, such as the ports of Toulon and Marseilles, were assaulted from the landward side.

Following its fire support missions during Operation *Neptune*, USS *Texas* returned to the Mediterranean in August 1944 to support the Operation *Dragoon* landings in southern France.

There were intermittent engagements between the Allied navies and remaining elements of the Atlantikwall through the summer of 1944. Fighting in Brittany lasted into September 1944, most notably for the port of Brest. The warship most closely associated with engagements of German coastal gun batteries was the HMS *Warspite*. On 25 August, it was assigned to soften up several of the forts on the western side of the Brest defences. *Warspite*'s commanding officer, Capt M.H.A. Kelsey, was well aware that several of the German gun batteries were encased in steel-reinforced concrete casemates which even his 15in. battleship guns would have a hard time penetrating. Rather than engage in a pointless duel with the German batteries, Kelsey decided to fire on them from off the north-west coast of Brittany, out of sight of the German fire control bunkers so that the guns could not retaliate.

The engagement began from a distance of 16 miles starting with a barrage of 57 rounds against Batterie Graf Spee. The spotting aircraft reported that the three exposed guns had been knocked out, but the fate of the one casemated gun was uncertain. As a result, *Warspite* turned its attention to the guns at Les Rospects, Batterie von Holtzendorf. This was followed by attacks on two of the old Vauban-era French forts, Fort Kéranoux and Fort Montbarey. Late in the afternoon, *Warspite* came under fire for the first time. Contrary to the spotter's report, only one of the Graf Spee guns had been damaged. The gun crews of Batterie Graf Spee spent two hours digging away debris from the initial bombardments and were able to make two of the

The most powerful guns on the Südwall were the two turreted 340mm guns of the 4.Batterie, MAA.682, originally installed by the French Navy in 1930 at Cap Cépet, to defend Toulon harbour. Turm Cäsar seen here was knocked out on 16 August by a direct hit by a 2,000lb bomb. During the subsequent gun duels, US and French warships fired some 1,084 rounds at both turrets. The surviving Turm Friedrich fired 218 rounds, scoring several straddles but without sinking any Allied warships.

HMS *Warspite* was widely used during the Normandy and Brittany campaign to provide heavy fire support for Allied forces. On 25 August 1944 it engaged Batterie Graf Spee near Lochrist suburb in support of US Army units besieging Brest in Brittany. This is depicted in this illustration by Darren Tan for the Osprey Campaign series book *Brittany 1944*. (© Osprey

Publishing Ltd)

guns operational again. In the meantime, Kriegsmarine survey posts on the coast spotted *Warspite* and began feeding ballistic data back to the Graf Spee fire control bunker. *Warspite* broke off the engagement based on the instructions from the American fire control officer. Both sides claimed victory. *Warspite* had completely shattered Fort Kéranoux, and seriously damaged the other targets. Batterie Graf Spee gleefully reported back to naval headquarters in Brest that it had fought off a British squadron.

In late August and early September, the Allies rolled up the German Atlantikwall defences in Upper Normandy and the Pas-de-Calais from the landward side including the heavily fortified ports of Le Havre and Boulogne. During the attack on Le Havre, the monitor HMS *Erebus* provided fire support. It engaged in a duel with Heeres-Küsten-Batterie (HKB: Army coastal battery) Goldbrunner, armed with three 170mm K.18 guns. The German guns hit the armoured bulge of *Erebus* at least twice on 5 September, encouraging the monitor to return to Portsmouth for repairs. On returning to Le Havre on 8 September, *Erebus* was hit by at least two salvoes but remained on station until 11 September when it returned to the dockyards for additional repairs and the removal of an unexploded 170mm projectile. Other ports such as Dieppe on the North Sea and the heavily fortified ports on the Bay of Biscay such as Royan and St Nazaire were isolated and placed under siege rather than being directly attacked.

The most intense fighting along the Atlantikwall in late 1944 occurred on 1 November 1944. The British 21st Army Group, supported by the Royal Navy, conducted Operation *Infatuate*, an amphibious landing on Walcheren island at the mouth of the Scheldt estuary in the Netherlands. This was intended to clear the Scheldt of German batteries that were preventing the Allies from using the port of Antwerp. Due to its strategic location, Walcheren island had been heavily fortified. The amphibious landings by the 4th Special Service Brigade against Westkapelle ran into a storm of gunfire from the German coastal batteries.

The Westkapelle landing zone was defended by three Kriegsmarine coastal artillery batteries of MAA.202. Marine-Küsten-Batterie (MKB: Navy coastal battery) Westkapelle of 6./MAA.202 was armed with four British 3.7in. anti-aircraft guns captured at Dunkirk and supported by two 75mm guns in open gun pits. The neighbouring MKB Zoutelande of 7./MAA.202 was armed with four 150mm TbtsK C/36 naval guns reinforced by two 75mm guns. MKB Domburg of 5./MAA.202 was farther inland near Zoutelande and had four French 220mm guns in open pits. Preliminary RAF strikes failed to neutralize the guns.

The landings were preceded by naval bombardment by HMS *Warspite* against MKB Domburg; the monitor HMS *Roberts* against MKB Zoutelande, and the monitor HMS *Erebus* against MKB Westkapelle. When the turret traverse on HMS *Erebus* failed, HMS *Roberts* was obliged to cover both

During the gun duel with HMS *Warspite* on 25 August 1944, only one of the four 280mm SK L/40 naval guns of Batterie Graf Spee of 5./MAA.262 was protected by a casemate. Batterie Hamburg would have had a similar appearance if its roofs had been completed. The chain mail draped in front of the gun was intended to offer splinter protection for the embrasure opening.

The Kriegsmarine coastal gun batteries near Westkapelle inflicted heavy losses on the Royal Navy gun support craft during the Operation *Infatuate* landings on Walcheren island during the Scheldt campaign on 1 November 1944. This is Landing Craft, Gun (Medium) 101, that was repeatedly hit by the guns of MKB Westkapelle. Its commander, Lt George Flamank, was awarded the DSC for his valiant actions that day.

gun batteries nearest the landing sites. The Royal Navy formation included a Close Support Squadron consisting of gun support craft and rocket craft that added to the fire against the bunkers as well as distracting the German gunners from the vulnerable infantry landing craft. In spite of the naval bombardment, the German coastal gun batteries continued to fire, mainly against the smaller and more vulnerable fire support craft. Of the 27 fire support craft taking part in the operation, ten were sunk and six were severely damaged. The sacrifice of the fire support craft helped get the landing force ashore. MKB Zoutelande ran out of ammunition before the Royal Marine Commandos arrived. MKB Westkapelle continued to fire and damaged two more tank landing craft during the landing phase. Both batteries were cleared by the Royal Marine Commandos by early afternoon; MKB Domburg, farther inland, was not captured until the next day. MAA.202 failed to stop the Westkapelle landings, but the two batteries were arguably the most destructive of any Atlantikwall coastal guns during the war.

The most dangerous Kriegsmarine gun battery on Walcheren was the 6.Batterie, MAA.202 of MKB Westkapelle. Its four Regelbau 671 casemates were armed with British 3.7in. anti-aircraft guns captured at Dunkirk. They inflicted heavy damage on Royal Navy craft during the 1 November battle. This is a post-war view after it was disarmed. (Nederlands Instituut voor Militaire Historie)

Most of the coastal gun batteries of the Atlantikwall saw little or no combat during the war. The Atlantikwall in Norway had 285 coastal gun batteries with over 1,500 guns but fired only about 200 rounds during the entire war, mainly against British small craft. The Atlantikwall in Denmark had 70 batteries with 365 guns but saw hardly any combat.

THE COMBATANTS

USS *TEXAS*

When deployed to the Normandy campaign in June 1944, the USS *Texas* was far from being the US Navy's most modern battleship. On the other hand, *Texas* had been extremely innovative for its time, and had often been at the cutting edge of naval gunfire development. When launched in March 1914, the USS *Texas* was the first battleship armed with the powerful 14in. gun.

The USS *Texas* off Newport News, Virginia on 15 March 1943 after its most recent refit. This is the configuration and camouflage scheme seen on the *Texas* during its action off Cherbourg.

Following its participation in the Mediterranean and European campaigns, USS *Texas* was dispatched to the Pacific theatre, taking part in the bombardment of Iwo Jima and Okinawa in 1945. It is seen here in January 1945 off the coast of Hawaii.

In its first overseas mission in May 1914, *Texas* was deployed with elements of the Atlantic Fleet off Veracruz in support of US operations to blockade arms shipments during the Mexican civil war. In 1918, *Texas* sailed for Great Britain and served with the Sixth Battle Squadron during the final months of World War I. Its only combat action of the war was an attempted torpedo attack by a German U-boat that *Texas* evaded.

On 9 March 1919, *Texas* launched a Sopwith Camel fighter from an improvised deck over its No. 2 turret to test the concept of using spotting planes to correct naval gunfire. This was the first time that this was attempted on a US Navy battleship, and it was the precursor of this innovative practice. It paved the way for the development of shipboard aircraft catapults to support spotter aircraft. In 1925, USS *Texas* underwent a substantial refit in the Norfolk Navy Yard to extend its service life. The 1922 Naval Limitation Treaty had imposed limits on the size of the US battleship force, and shortage of funds meant that the Navy would have to operate *Texas* for a decade longer than originally planned. One of the most significant changes was the replacement of coal-fuelled boilers with more modern oil-fuelled boilers. This freed up considerable space and a more substantial plotting room was created below the waterline in front of Boiler Room B-2. The refit also included additional armour, enhanced torpedo bulges, new tripod masting and superstructure improvements. Its torpedo tubes were removed and many of its secondary 5in. guns on the lower deck were removed. An aircraft catapult was installed over the No. 3 turret during the modernization effort. In the 1930s, *Texas* hosted a trio of Vought O3U-3 Corsair floatplanes that served for spotting duties.

Texas was the flagship of the United States Fleet in the late 1920s. It underwent a second refit in the spring of 1931 in the New York Navy Yard and was subsequently assigned as the Flagship of Battle Division 1 in the Pacific, stationed at San Diego. Another round of refits was undertaken in the Puget Sound Yards in early 1935 that included enhanced anti-aircraft defences. In 1937, further anti-aircraft guns were added in the form of eight 1.1in. (28mm) AA guns in two quadruple mounts. In 1937, it returned to the US Atlantic Squadron, serving again as flagship.

VICE ADMIRAL CARLETON F. BRYANT

Vice Admiral Carleton F. Bryant commanded Bombardment Group 2 on 25 June 1944, using the USS *Texas* as his flagship for the mission. Bryant was born on 29 November 1892 in New York City, attended the US Naval Academy at Annapolis starting in 1910 and was commissioned in 1914. He served on the battleship USS *Wyoming* during the Veracruz Expedition in autumn 1914, and later took part in naval operations in Europe in 1918 during World War I. During the inter-war years, he held a variety of positions and attended a number of professional schools.

Bryant was promoted to Captain on 1 July 1940, becoming the Assistant Director, Office of Naval Intelligence. Bryant assumed command of the battleship USS *Arkansas* in April 1941, taking part in numerous convoy missions as well as bombardment support for Operation *Torch* off Casablanca, Morocco, in November 1942. He was promoted to Rear Admiral in May 1943, assuming command of Battleship Division 5, Atlantic Fleet. Bryant participated in the planning of Operation *Neptune* and commanded the Gunfire Support Group of Assault Force O off Omaha Beach on D-Day. Following the Normandy campaign, he served as Commander of the Center Support Group of the Western Naval Task Force during the Operation *Dragoon* amphibious invasion of southern France in August 1944. Having won numerous awards and decorations, he returned to the United States in September 1944 as Commander, Fleet Operational Training Command, United States Atlantic Fleet until his retirement in 1946. He died on 11 April 1987, aged 94.

CAPTAIN CHARLES A. BAKER

Captain Charles A. Baker served as commanding officer of the USS *Texas* during the 25 June 1944 mission. He was born in Lynchburg, Virginia, on 27 September 1893, attended the US Naval Academy starting in 1912 and was commissioned as an Ensign in June 1916. He did not see overseas service in World War I; his first battleship experience came in 1920–22 aboard the USS *Tennessee*. After varied postings in the inter-war years, he served as Executive Officer of the battleship USS *Maryland* in July 1940. In May 1941, he was assigned as Assistant Naval Attaché of the American Embassy in London. On 10 March 1944 he assumed command of USS *Texas*, and remained in command until August 1945 including the operations of the USS *Texas* in the Pacific during the bombardments of Iwo Jima and Okinawa. As a Rear Admiral, he served on the staff of the Office of the Assistant Secretary of the Navy until his retirement in 1949. He died in 1970 at age 77.

Rear Adm Carleton F. Bryant (left), commander of Bombardment Group 2 during the 25 June mission and Capt Charles A. Baker, commanding officer of USS *Texas*, stand next to the dud German 240mm projectile that penetrated into the officers' quarters on *Texas* without exploding.

BATTLESHIP FIRE CONTROLS

Although not as visible as the many external changes, USS *Texas* underwent continual improvements in its gun fire control systems through the inter-war years. Compared to coastal gun batteries, warships face a substantially more difficult challenge in the accuracy of their gunnery. The principal difference is that the warship is moving when it fires. As a result, the ship fire control must compensate for the continual motion of the ship in multiple axes: pitching back and forth, rolling from side to side, and yawing in bearing. These movements can occur even when the ship is at anchor; they are amplified when the ship is in movement. The other aspects of naval gunnery are similar to those of coastal guns such as accurate range-finding to the target, accurate determination of the target's azimuth and height, compensation for factors such as weather, propellant temperature, barrel wear and other ballistic changes.

The eyes of USS *Texas* were its numerous optical and radar sensors: (1) Mark 4 Mod 3 gun director; (2) Mark 21 Gun Director for 14in. guns; (3) Mark 50 Gun Director for 3in. guns; (4) Mark 6 Mod 7 Gun Director for 5in. guns; (5) Main Battery Lookout; (6) Mark 20 Mod 1 Gun Director for 14in. guns; (7) SG Surface-search Radar; (8) Mark 3 Fire Control Radar; (9) Spot 1; (10) Rangefinder; (11) Spot 2; (12) Mark 3 Fire Control Radar; (13) Mark 20 Mod 1 Gun Director for 14in. guns; (14) Mark 6 Mod 7 Gun Director for 5in. guns; (15) SG Surface-Search Radar; (16) SK Air Search Radar; (17) Mark 50 Gun Director for 3in. guns. (Author)

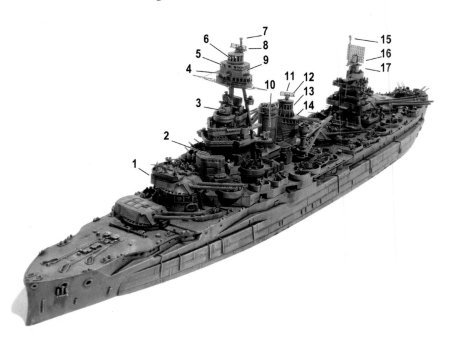

USS *TEXAS* (BB-35)

Technical data		Propulsion	Babcock & Wilcox oil-fired boilers,
Commissioned	12 March 1914		steam turbines
Builder	Newport News Shipbuilding	Speed	21 knots @ 28,000 shaft horsepower
Crew	98 officers, 1,625 enlisted men	Endurance	15,400 nautical miles @ 10 knots
Length	573ft	Main battery	10 x 14 in./45cal
Beam	106ft	Secondary battery	6 x 5in./51cal
Displacement	30,350 (34,000 loaded) tons	Anti-aircraft	10 x 3in.; 40 x 40mm; 42 x 20mm
Armour	10–12in. (main belt); 4–9in. (turrets)		

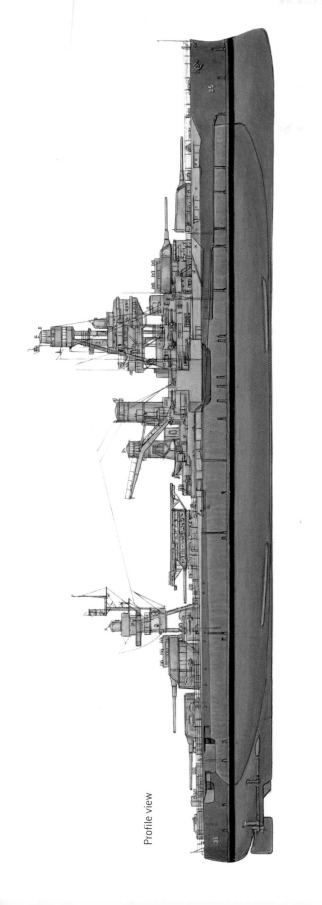

Profile view

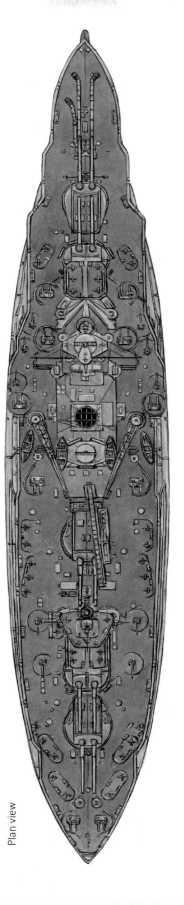

Plan view

14IN. 45CAL TWO-GUN TURRET, USS *TEXAS*

Technical data

Guns	14in. 45 Mk 12 Mod 1	Elevation	-5 to +15 degrees
Turret rotating weight	532 tons	Elevation speed	4 degrees per second
Gun weight	142,490lb each	Traverse speed	100 degrees per minute
Recoil weight	158,000lb per gun	Projectile weight	1,500lb (AP); 1,275lb (HC)
Trunnion pressure	930,000lb @ 15 degrees	Powder charge	420lb
Max. powder pressure	18 tons per square inch	Muzzle velocity (AP)	2,600fps (AP); 2,735fps (HC)
		Max range	23,000yd (AP); 23,500yd (HC)

The data from a battleship's radars, rangefinders, azimuth indicators and other sensors were fed to the plotting room where it was integrated with the ship's motion sensors to calculate ballistic solutions for the guns. World War II photos of these rooms are rare due to the secrecy of the advanced computing equipment. This is the plotting room on the USS *Missouri* (BB-63).

Attempts to compensate for ship motion in fire control began in the early 20th century with techniques to overcome the effects of rolling, an important factor since battleships often fired broadsides where rolling was a potential source of inaccuracy. Technological innovations in this period, such as gyros, were used to create devices to monitor the movement of the ship in relation to true vertical. Accuracy in range-finding was addressed by early wide-base coincidence optical rangefinders, pioneered by Barr & Stroud in Britain. The United States Navy followed suit and the USS *Texas* was fitted with 20ft Bausch & Lomb turret rangefinders.

Another major complication of fire control at sea was the need to determine the continual change of the target location along the line-of-sight, called the range rate, and the rate across the line-of-sight, called deflection. The Royal Navy's Dumaresq course-solver first appeared in 1905, termed a component-solver in the US Navy. Further improvements, for example gyro systems to compensate for motion, led to the development of sophisticated plotting tables such as the Dreyer table during World War I. Devices which used the analytic approach to determine range rate like the Dreyer table were superseded by analogue computers using the synthetic approach, such as the Ford range-keeper that was tested on USS *Texas* in 1916. It was adopted

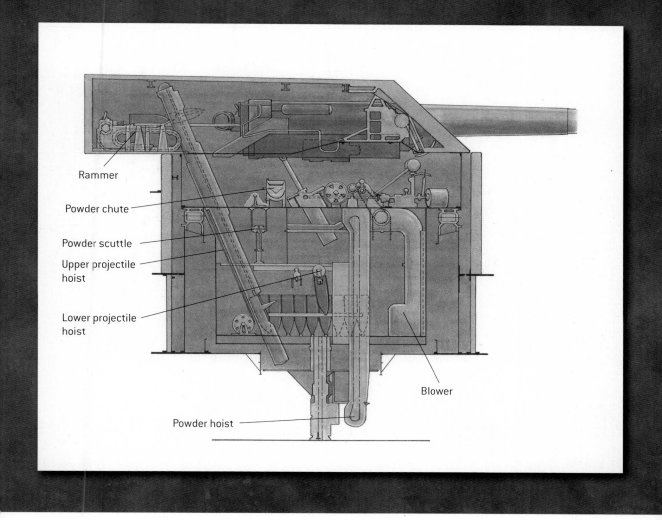

Rammer

Powder chute

Powder scuttle

Upper projectile hoist

Lower projectile hoist

Blower

Powder hoist

in 1918 and upgraded after the war with a graphic plotter. It was supplemented with a Ford converter that converted gun range into gun elevation.

As these devices increased in sophistication, so too did methods evolve to transfer the gunnery data from the fire control centre to the guns. In its earliest form, this was usually a telephone system. In time, means were developed to transmit the data more precisely to the guns that would be provided to the crew via dial displays. General Electric developed its self-synchronous motors (selsyns) to automate gun control, later called synchro in the US Navy. In the years before World War I, efforts were made to unify the data dissemination and the control over multiple guns. A critical innovation was the use of a director to control the ship's batteries from a single position.

On large US Navy warships such as battleships, fire control was redundant due to the risk of battle damage. USS *Texas* had two Ford Mk 1 devices in the plotting room under the conning tower, two masthead control positions and a control tower built into the conning tower. In the late 1920s, the US Navy began to adopt a next-generation, consolidated fire control system. The *Texas* and its sister ship *New York* were the first battleships to receive this upgrade, consisting of Mk XX directors in each

US NAVY 14IN. AMMUNITION

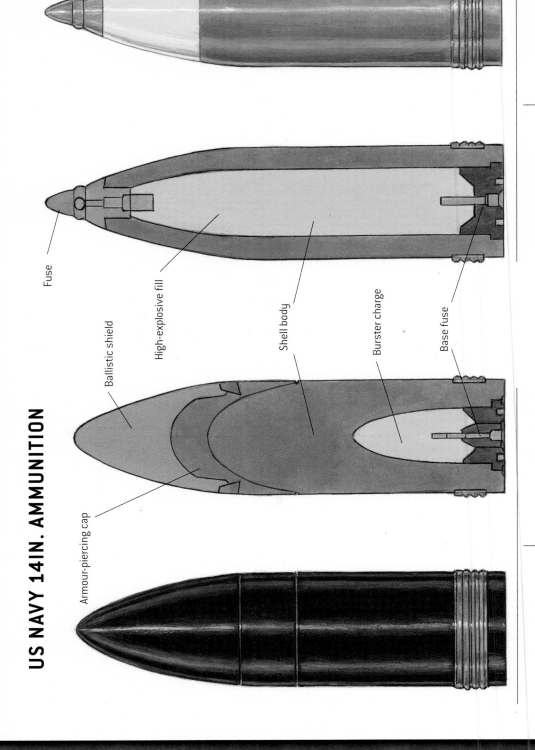

Fuse

Ballistic shield

High-explosive fill

Shell body

Burster charge

Base fuse

Armour-piercing cap

14in. High-Capacity Mark 19 Mods 1–6

14in. Armour Piercing Mark 20 Mod 1

top, a Mark XXI director in the fire-control tower, and a Mk IX Mod 3 stable vertical and Mk 1 range-keeper in the plotting room.

USS *Texas* again served as the testbed for naval innovation when it was fitted with an experimental radar in late 1938. This was part of a broader US Navy effort to develop shipboard radars, intended for air search to help the battleship defend itself against air attack. Two different types were under consideration: RCA's CXZ on *Texas* and the Naval Research Labs, XAF radar on BB34 *New York*. Trials of the two radars in 1939 concluded that the XAF had longer range while the CXZ had better definition. This led to the development of the next generation of shipboard radar, the RCA CXAM air search radar. At the time of the US entry into World War II, only 20 of these radars had been deployed. *Texas* was the first ship in the Atlantic Squadron to have radar permanently installed on board, receiving its CXAM-1 in October 1941 during a refit at the Norfolk Navy Yard. The FC radar, later called the Mark 3, was introduced on USS *Texas* with one on the foretop and one on the mid-ship defence tower. During the February 1943 refit in Boston Navy Yard, a new SG surface-search radar was added to the foretop. The *Texas* also had its Combat Information Centre (CIC) substantially modernized during this refit.

USS *Texas* continued to have changes and upgrades through the early years of World War II. The threat of air attack led to numerous changes in its anti-aircraft gun configuration. The 1.1in. quad anti-aircraft mount adopted in 1940 was not successful, and was removed during the June 1943 refit in Boston Navy Yard in favour of ten 40mm quad Bofors mounts. In addition, *Texas* received increasing numbers of 20mm Oerlikon automatic cannon for air defence totalling 16 in 1941, 38 in 1942 and 44 by 1944.

With the outbreak of war in Europe in September 1939, the US Navy began naval patrols out into the Atlantic, with USS *Texas* taking part. Although *Texas* did not participate in the early Pacific campaigns, some of its guns did play a role. The US Marine garrison on Wake Island was equipped with six 5in. guns that had been removed from *Texas* during its 1926 refit. On 11 December 1941, Battery L, on Peale islet, sank the Japanese destroyer IJN *Hayate* at 4,000yd with two direct hits to her magazines; the detonation of the magazines sank the ship in only two minutes. This was the first Japanese surface warship sunk by US forces during the war, and a curious link between *Texas* and coastal gun batteries.

Texas undertook patrols to Iceland and the Panama Canal in early 1942. In its first major combat mission of the war, *Texas* served with the Western Task Force landing elements of the 9th Division in the capture of Casablanca. The plan did not include a pre-landing bombardment since there was some hope that the French garrison would enthusiastically switch sides. This proved to be overly optimistic and the French garrison began fighting back. The 60th Infantry, 9th Division had an attached SFCP which called for fire support against a French munitions dump near Port Lyautey. For the first time during the war, USS *Texas* fired its 14in. guns in anger starting at 1343 on 8 November 1942, firing 59 rounds at a range of 16,500yd. Another fire support mission was conducted on 10 November against a French motorized column. Curiously enough, that afternoon a Kingfisher spotter aircraft from USS *Texas* attacked a French tank column that was attacking US troops near Port Lyautey. It dropped a modified depth charge, blowing up one tank and overturning two others. These were probably World War I-vintage Renault FT tanks. The 14in. guns of the *Texas* were credited with several other kills against French tanks during its fire support missions, hurling some of them into the air according to army forward observers.

Texas continued its convoy escort duties through 1943. In April 1944 it arrived in Scotland for preparations associated with Operation *Neptune*, the forthcoming Normandy amphibious operation. Its mission for Operation *Neptune* was to provide fire support at Omaha Beach.

SPOTTING FOR THE GUNS

By 1944, fire control tactics in support of amphibious operations had changed. Although *Texas* had used its own Kingfisher floatplanes for spotting duties off Morocco in 1942, this practice was halted for Operation *Neptune*. During the Operation *Husky* landings on Sicily in July 1943, ship-based floatplanes were found to be extremely vulnerable to enemy flak and enemy fighter aircraft due to their slow speed. As a result, the Royal Navy proposed using land-based fighters, specifically Spitfires and Seafires based at Lee-on-Solent. The US Navy floatplanes were flown ashore and the pilots converted to Spitfire Mk Vb in a consolidated squadron, VCS-7.

The Spitfires operated in groups of two, one aircraft to do the spotting and a 'weaver' to keep an eye out for German fighters. The use of single-seat fighters based in England was an effective but inefficient method of targeting as later related by Vice Admiral Morton L. Deyo in an after-action report:

> The greatest handicap was the short range of the Spitfires. Basing at Lee-on-the-Solent, roughly 100 miles from the Normandy coast, each flight would be able to remain with us a bare 45 minutes in good weather before returning to base for fuel. They would, in fact, be at their maximum operating limit. They worked in pairs, each spotting plane

The Spitfire Mk Vb fighters of VCS-7 operated in pairs during spotting missions as seen in this illustration. One aircraft performed the spotting mission while the second fighter served as escort in the event of German

fighters in the area. (Author)

having its 'weavers' to watch for enemy planes. There would be another pair en route to and from base and still two more fueling at base. That made a total of six planes for each spotting mission; a costly business and a makeshift. But lacking longer-range planes or aircraft carriers, it had to do.

The second method for spotting was the SFCP (shore fire control party), the US equivalent of the British FOB (forward observation bombardment party). The SFCP had been used by the US Army during Operation *Torch* and subsequent amphibious operations in the Mediterranean. Each SFCP consisted of one army and one navy officer, and 12 enlisted men. It was organized into two sections, an army forward observer section led by an army officer, and a naval liaison section led by an NGLO (naval gunnery liaison officer). Every ship participating in the bombardment was assigned an army artillery officer who maintained up-to-date information about the position of Allied troops and determined the desirability of firing at any given target. Each US Army division was assigned nine SFCPs on the scale of one SFCP per assault battalion. A navy gunfire officer was attached to each divisional headquarters in charge of all SFCPs in the division. The SFCP trained with its corresponding ship prior to D-Day. Although each SFCP was assigned to a specific ship, these units could operate with other ships when the need arose.

To begin a bombardment, the SFCP made contact with its firing ship via radio link and then designated a target by reference to a grid. Once the target was approved on board the ship by the army liaison officer, the SFCP observed the fall-of-shot and corrected fire by a means of the clock method described previously. In general, the spotting aircraft were used to locate targets-of-opportunity, most often German artillery batteries. The SFCPs were most commonly used to bring fire on targets impeding the advance of their associated infantry assault battalion.

US Navy VCS-7 pilots were briefed before flying a gunfire spotting mission. This was a coordinated Anglo-American effort as is evident from those present including (from left to right): Wing Commander Robert J. Hardiman, RAF, Commanding Allied Spotter Pilots; Ensign Robert J. Adams, USNR; Major Noel East, British Army Intelligence; Lieutenant Harris Hammersmith, Jr, USNR; and Captain John Ruscoe, Royal Artillery, Gunnery Liaison Officer.

BATTERIE HAMBURG

Batterie Hamburg was armed with four 240mm SK L/40 (Schnellladekanone Länge: Fast-loading gun, Calibre/40). When this gun entered production at Krupp in Essen in the late 1890s, it was the first large-calibre Kriegsmarine gun to employ brass propellant cases. It armed the Kaiser and Wittelsbach classes of battleships as well as the Fürst Bismarck and Prinz Heinrich classes of armoured cruisers. The four guns of Batterie Hamburg originally equipped the armoured cruiser SMS *Fürst Bismarck*, commissioned in April 1900. It was withdrawn from fleet service in 1915 and became a training ship. As a result, the guns were removed to serve in coastal fortifications.

The Kriegsmarine had begun coastal gun conversions using the 210mm SK L/50 warship guns by developing a Bettungsschießgerüst (ship platform mount) that could accommodate a single gun. This rotated on a fixed pivot mount under the front of the gun and a set of wheels at the rear of the frame, riding on a circular rail to assist in traversing such a substantial assembly. The first was emplaced with Batterie Plantagen at the Swinemünde naval base on the Baltic coast.

Eight of the surplus 240mm SK L/40 guns were earmarked for coastal defence with Batterie Skagerrak on Sylt island in the North Sea, and Batterie Hamburg at Norderney in the Frisian islands on the North Sea. Eighteen other guns were allotted to the Army for use on the Western Front. These were expected to be mounted on the same type of Bettungsgerüst as the coastal guns, but the Army was not pleased with the expensive process of deploying these guns in a fixed position. Instead, they were mounted on a new dual-purpose Eisenbahn und Bettungsgerüst (EuB: railroad and platform mount) that could either be rail mobile or placed quickly in a fixed position. These were later designated as the Theodor Karl railroad guns.

The guns assigned to Batterie Hamburg at the Norderney naval base were installed in kettle gun pits. They were assigned to Marine-Artillerie-Abteilung.126 which operated other coastal defence guns there. They remained in service there until 6 June 1940 when they were dismantled and transferred to Blankenberghe, Belgium. This was short-lived when Berlin decided to use the guns to create a new battery for the defence of the port of Cherbourg. This coastal defence programme pre-dated the Atlantikwall programme and reflected the traditional German naval doctrine that emphasized the defence of key ports. This was one of the first German coastal gun batteries to appear in Lower Normandy during the war.

Construction of the new Marine-Küsten-Batterie Hamburg began on 25 July 1940 on the southern outskirts of the village of Fermanville, located inland from Cap Lévy to the east of Cherbourg. The initial design incorporated four Kesselbettung Regelbau Bh.4 kettle gun pits. These were essentially similar to the concrete gun pits used in World War I. Construction of the gun pits was completed in September 1940 and the parts for the four guns began to be assembled at the site. The new mountings added an elementary 5mm steel splinter shield at the front and top of the gun. Construction of the gun positions was followed by the construction of eight ammunition bunkers, four personnel bunkers, a generator building and four 2cm Flak positions. The battery's fire control post (Leitstand) was created by taking over a chateau on the Tôt du Haut road near Fermanville overlooking the sea. The optical rangefinder was placed on the roof with a protective wall. Subsequently, an underground bunker was constructed nearby to contain the plotting room and this was completed in 1941. This construction was all undertaken by Kriegsmarine construction units.

Batterie Hamburg eventually became part of Marine-Artillerie-Abteilung.260, headquartered in Cherbourg. MAA.260 was an unusually large command with ten naval gun batteries, all under the command of Kapitänleutnant MA Karl Weise. It stretched from Batterie Gréville west of Cherbourg to Batterie Longues-sur-Mer east of the future Omaha Beach. Due to this overextension, in late 1943 some of its batteries were put under the direction of army coastal artillery battalions. In 1944, Batterie Hamburg was commanded by Oberleutnant MA Rudi Ernst Max Gelbhaar and the battery consisted of about 250 naval personnel.

Once the basic layout of Batterie Hamburg was completed in 1940, there was very little new construction work until the summer of 1943. At this point, the gun positions began a major reconstruction under Hitler's Schartenstand Programm. Undertaken by Organization Todt (a civil and military engineering organization), the new construction work used a variety of labour, including Soviet and Italian prisoners-of-war as well as French and Belgian men impressed into labour service.

A detailed aerial view of the north-western corner of Batterie Hamburg taken after its surrender in late June 1944. Visible here are Turm 1 (1); the incomplete M 178 Leitstand (2); the western Belgian Krupp 7.5cm K.235 (b) field gun emplacement (3); the incomplete Turm 4 gun casemate (4); and the northernmost war-booty French 75mm Flak M.36 (f) gun position (5).

A general aerial view of Batterie Hamburg looking eastward and identifying the four gun casemates by their number. The gun pits in the lower right of the photo are the six war-booty French 75mm Flak M.36(f) anti-aircraft guns. For some reason, the US Army censor has obscured the Viaduc de Fermanville that spanned the Vallée des Moulins south-east of Batterie Hamburg.

The new gun bunkers at Fermanville used a Sonderkonstruktion (SK) design, that is a non-standard design instead of an existing Regelbau design. This was done for several reasons including the relatively uncommon type of gun and the decision to build the casemate to the heavier Standard A (Baustärke A) construction with 3m thicker roof and walls. In addition, the special design incorporated an unusually large ammunition bunker

An overhead view of Turm 1 of Batterie Hamburg taken after the fighting. This casemate was only partially complete and the wall on the left side of the gun was knocked down. This provided more traverse to the south-west to allow the gun to fire on approaching US Army units.

KRIEGSMARINE 240MM AMMUNITION

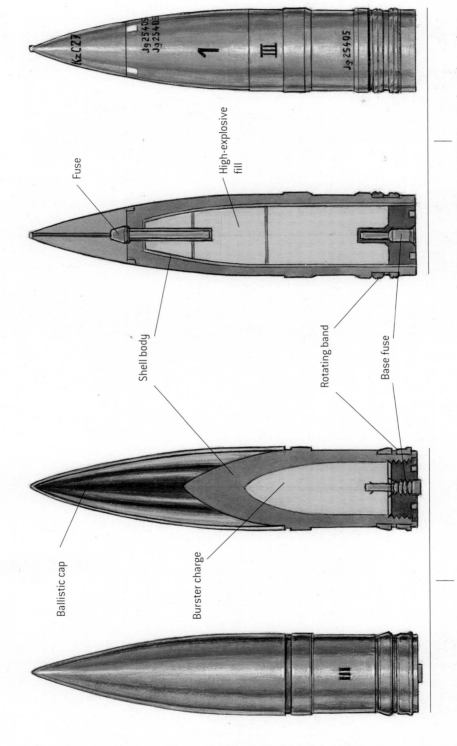

Ballistic cap

Burster charge

Shell body

Fuse

High-explosive fill

Rotating band

Base fuse

240mm Panzergranate L/2.6m Bdz (armour piercing with base fuse)

240mm Sprengranate L/4.2 Bdz u. Kz (m.Hb) umg (high-explosive with base and nose fuses; modified)

A view of Turm 2 of Batterie Hamburg being inspected by US Army officers after it was surrendered. It still lacks the intended roof over the gun, featuring a camouflage net instead. As can be seen, this gun casemate appears to have suffered little or no damage during the 25 June engagement.

at the rear of the casemate called the Bauteil B/Muni-Bereitschaftsraum that could accommodate 1,340 rounds. The bunker included a hoist system to facilitate reloading the gun. These massive casemates required 2,800 cubic metres of concrete weighing some 6,720 tonnes, plus a further 23 tonnes of rebar and other steel components.

The plans for these new gun casemates were not approved until mid-February 1944. As a result, the work in the second half of 1943 focused on other installations around the strongpoint including two separate ammunition bunkers. Construction of the first three casemates began in February 1944, followed by the fourth in March. Due to their delayed start, Organization Todt reported to Berlin that the four casemates could not be completed until June 1944 at the earliest. This was further delayed in March when a typhus outbreak occurred among the 500 Soviet prisoners of war working on the site. Further delays occurred in April when the steel beams needed for the roof failed to arrive, forcing Organization Todt to send a search party into France to track them down.

The month of April 1944 saw the most intense level of Atlantikwall construction in Normandy due to the expectation that an invasion would occur in May 1944. As a result, there was a continual shortage of construction supplies, especially steel rebar. The missing roof beams were finally located by late May 1944, but they had not been completely prepared according to the plans and so required further modification. The enormous scale of the Batterie Hamburg construction programme accounted for nearly a third of all the concrete required for naval fortification efforts on the eastern side of the Cotentin peninsula in 1944.

The other major structure planned for the battery was an M 178 Leitstand. This was the standard Kriegsmarine fire control bunker for heavy coastal gun batteries.

OBERLEUTNANT DER MARINE-ARTILLERIE DER RESERVE RUDI GELBHAAR

Oberleutnant Rudi Gelbhaar commanded Batterie Hamburg in June 1944. He was born in Falkenberg, Saxony, on 24 January 1915 and entered the Kriegsmarine in December 1934. He was commissioned to the rank of Leutnant (MA) on 1 February 1940, and appointed as assistant commander of Batterie Hamburg of Marine-Artillerie-Abteilung 260 in Cherbourg in July 1940. He was awarded the Iron Cross II Class on 11 November 1940, presumably for his leadership when Batterie Hamburg fired on Royal Navy warships that were bombarding Cherbourg on the night of 10–11 October 1940. On 1 April 1942, he advanced to the rank of Oberleutnant, was awarded the Iron Cross I Class and became battery commander. The circumstance for this second award is not clear, but may have been due to his leadership of Batterie Hamburg rather than a specific combat action.

For his actions during the duel with Bombardment Group 2, he was awarded the Knight's Cross of the Iron Cross on 26 June 1944. The citation for the award stated: 'Yesterday, Batterie Hamburg, commanded by Oberleutnant of the Marine-Artillerie Gelbhaar, sunk two enemy cruisers in the Cherbourg area while itself being under heavy artillery fire. Furthermore another four cruisers were heavily damaged by [other] Marine Batterien in the same area during the preceding days.' He surrendered the battery to the US 4th Infantry Division on 28 June and remained a prisoner of war through to April 1946. Little has been published about his post-war life. He died in Wetzlar, Hesse, at age 87 on 24 November 2002.

Oberleutnant MA Rudi Ernst Max Gelbhaar, commander of Batterie Hamburg.

This structure would have required a further 2,300 cubic metres of concrete weighing 5,040 tonnes, plus 12 tonnes of steel rebar and 5.3 tonnes of structural steel for doors, roof beams and other parts. Although work began, it was never completed due to the shortages of manpower and construction supplies. Instead, the improvised Leitstand based on the chateau on the Tôt du Haut road continued to be used for this purpose.

While the gun casemates were under construction, other aspects of the site were improved. The number of 20mm Flak positions increased from four to seven. A battery of six war-booty French 75mm Flak M 17/34 (f) was installed on the south-west corner of the site. Two war-booty Belgian Krupp 7.5cm K.235 (b) field guns were installed for target illumination and site defence. The fortified battery was classified as Stützpunkt 234 (Strongpoint 234) and extensive self-defence features were added including small machine-gun Tobruks, barbed wire, roadblocks and other defences.

One of the curious outcomes of the Schartenstand Programm at Batterie Hamburg was that it reduced Allied anxiety over the threat that it posed to the forthcoming Operation *Neptune* landings. When Allied planners added Utah Beach to the list of five D-Day invasion beaches in early 1944, they believed that the Batterie Hamburg guns could reach the transport area off the beach where the transport ships loaded the landing troops into the landing craft. As the gun casemates took shape at Batterie Hamburg in the spring of 1944, Allied intelligence analysts realized that the embrasures limited the traverse of the guns to the north to cover eastern approaches to Cherbourg, and could no longer fire south-east towards Utah Beach. As a result, Batterie Hamburg was removed from the list of German batteries slated for heavy bomber attack during the pre-invasion stage.

INTO COMBAT

Batterie Hamburg claimed to have shot down an Allied aircraft on 11 March 1944. The first significant air attack occurred on 12 April when the site was strafed by Allied fighters. On 23 May the battery was attacked by 20 RAF Typhoons which dropped some bombs on the southern side of the site; one aircraft was claimed by the battery's flak as a 'probable'. The following day, the site was strafed again by two Mustangs. A large bombing raid was conducted in the late afternoon of 27 May apparently aimed at the nearby radar site. There were no losses and the battery flak claimed to have hit at least one Allied aircraft.

By the time of the D-Day landings on 6 June 1944, only three of the four gun casemates were nearing completion. Turm 1 in the north-east had its gun pit and portions of its wall complete but no substantial work on its ammunition bunker. Turm 2 and Turm 3 were the most complete except for the lack of their concrete roofs. Turm 4 in the north-west corner was only partially started with a gun pit, partial walls and a secondary ammunition bunker finished.

A view of the left side of Turm 2 of Batterie Hamburg. This casemate was largely complete except for its roof. The door evident to the right offered access into the rear ammunition rooms.

In early 1944, Batterie Hamburg was reinforced by a battery of six 75mm anti-aircraft guns. This particular example is one of the older Flak M 17/34 (f), the German designation for war-booty French 'Canon de 75mm contre aeronefs sur remorque Schneider'. These had been modernized in the mid-1930s and impressed into German service after their capture in 1940. (Swan/Rudziak)

Following the D-Day invasion, construction at the site ground to a halt since the Cotentin peninsula was quickly cut off from the rest of France by a US Army advance out of the Utah Beach area. Further construction was impossible due to a lack of sufficient steel rebar and concrete. This left Batterie Hamburg in an awkward state since none of the gun batteries had overhead cover while, at the same time, the partial construction of the casemates prevented the guns from being traversed to the south to enable them to fire at advancing US Army troops.

The 75mm Flak battery lost one of its guns on 11 June when a shell burst in its barrel, presumably due to faulty ammunition. The first known action by Batterie Hamburg since D-Day occurred on the afternoon of 16 June against Allied warships of Task Force 125 that were operating off the coast. On 19 June Batterie Hamburg and the neighbouring Batterie Landemer fired at other Allied warships shortly after midnight without any hits. On 20 June, many of the crews of Batterie Blankenese arrived at Batterie Hamburg after their battery was abandoned; they reinforced the gun crews there.

The only significant air raid against Batterie Hamburg after D-Day occurred on 20 June when the US 9th Air Force staged a mission with 18 P-47 Thunderbolt fighter-bombers dropping 36 500lb bombs. A barracks was destroyed and one bomb struck a 20mm Flak position, destroying the gun and killing four of the crew. One bomb lodged into one of the casemates but failed to detonate.

The MAA.260 headquarters in Cherbourg instructed Organization Todt to knock down the walls in Turm 1 to permit the gun to traverse southward. This allowed one of the battery's guns to bombard the approaching American troops starting on 20 June. The five 75mm Flak guns also were used to fire on approaching US troops during the fighting around Valognes to the south-east.

When German troops retreated from the neighbouring town of Saint-Pierre-Église, one of the battery's officers led a small team to retrieve abandoned equipment to reinforce Batterie Hamburg. This included a few 50mm PaK 38 and 75mm PaK 40 anti-tank guns as well as some trucks, ammunition and food.

THE STRATEGIC SITUATION

The duel between the USS *Texas* and Batterie Hamburg took part at the culmination of the Cherbourg campaign. The initial operational objective of the First US Army after the Normandy landings was to capture the port of Cherbourg to provide the Allies with a major logistical supply base in France. After cutting off the Cotentin peninsula on 17 June 1944, the VII Corps began a steady advance northward towards Cherbourg against heavy German resistance. The Wehrmacht had considered Cherbourg to be a potential Allied objective, and so the Cotentin peninsula was heavily fortified. The eastern and western coasts of the Cotentin peninsula had numerous heavy gun batteries to discourage Allied landings near Cherbourg. The port had numerous coastal gun batteries, and Festung (Fortress) Cherbourg was defended on the landward side by a string of fortifications called the Cherbourg Landfront.

Shortly after the VII Corps cut off the peninsula, Rear Adm A.G. Kirk, commander of the Western Task Force, offered naval gunfire support to the Army. Major General J. Lawton 'Lightning Joe' Collins, the VII Corps commander, responded that he wanted the Navy to deal with the 20 casemated batteries on either side of Cherbourg, however, there was a major storm in the Channel on the night of 19–20 June that forced Allied warships back to ports in England. The storm wrecked the new Mulberry harbour that had been erected off Omaha Beach, making the capture of Cherbourg all the more essential. The senior Allied naval commander, Adm Bertram Ramsay, after discussing the plan with the First US Army commander, Lt Gen Omar Bradley, instructed Kirk to prepare for a bombardment, tentatively scheduled for 24 June. On 22 June, Col Fred Campbell, the VII Corps artillery liaison officer, consulted with the Navy about the targets.

By 21 June, the VII Corps had reached the Cherbourg Landfront and began a concerted attack to penetrate the defences. Hitler insisted that Cherbourg be held to the last man, and there were expectations that the port could hold out for months due to extensive defences. In reality, the German infantry divisions defending the Cotentin peninsula had suffered such heavy casualties in the first three weeks of the fighting that the Landfront could barely be held. On 22–23 June, US VII Corps comprehensively breached the Landfront defences and Gen Collins asked the Navy if they could begin the bombardment on 24 June.

Rear Admiral Morton Deyo, commanding Task Group 129, organized two bombardment groups for the mission. Bombardment Group 1 (TG 129.1, call-sign Gaslight) was led by Deyo himself and was composed of the heavy cruisers USS *Tuscaloosa* and *Quincy*, the Royal Navy light cruisers HMS *Enterprise* and *Glasgow*, as well as six destroyers. This formation was assigned targets on the western side of Cherbourg as well as the port defences themselves. The targets on the eastern side of Cherbourg were the mission of Bombardment Group 2 (TG 129.2, call-sign Trailmate) led by Rear Adm Carleton F. Bryant. The Cherbourg bombardment mission was

The battleship USS *Arkansas* in early 1944, probably in Portland harbour. This ship was from the Wyoming class and was commissioned in 1913. It was armed with 12in. guns and its fire controls were not as advanced as those on *Texas*.

TRAILMATE: TASK GROUP 129.2 COMPOSITION

USS *Texas* (BB-35)

USS *Arkansas* (BB-33)

USS *Barton* (DD-722)

USS *Hobson* (DD-464)

USS *Laffey* (DD-724)

USS *O'Brien* (DD-725)

USS *Plunkett* (DD-431)

Mine Squadron 7 (TG 125.9.3)

USS *Forrest* (DD-461) served with Task Group 129.7 on 24 June when Turm 3 of Batterie Hamburg was knocked out. It is seen here on 20 March 1944 refuelling from the USS *Guadalcanal* (CVE-60) near the Azores.

detailed in Op Plan #7-44 and was issued on the morning of 24 June. Bombardment Group 2 is the focus of this duel.

The two bombardment groups began to sortie from Portland on the afternoon of 24 June, but the mission was called off in the late afternoon since the battleship *Arkansas* was still in Plymouth along with one of the minesweeper squadrons that was needed to clear the channels to the bombardment stations. As a result, the mission was rescheduled for 25 June.

While discussions were under way concerning the bombardment mission, minesweeping operations were carried out to facilitate any further naval operations around Cherbourg. Task Group 129.7 under Commander John Zahn on the destroyer USS *Walke* was clearing mines off the eastern coast of the Cotentin peninsula. Frequent minesweeping off Cherbourg was necessary as the Luftwaffe was conducting sporadic night mine-laying operations. Zahn's force consisted of over a dozen US and Royal Navy minesweepers, escorted by the destroyers USS *Walke* and USS *Forrest*. On 22 June, the minesweeper force came under fire from an unidentified German battery with the destroyers responding in a short and inconclusive engagement. The minesweeping operations continued on 23 June without any further incidents.

On 24 June, the minesweeping group returned with six US Navy and six Royal Navy minesweepers. The force rounded Pointe de Barfleur, advancing westward and closer to Cherbourg. Around 1356, Batterie Hamburg began firing from a range of over 20,000yd, later joined by the neighbouring Batterie Brommy to the south-west. The first salvo disappeared without a trace; the trajectory may have been so flat that no splashes were seen. When *Walke* spotted a second set of flashes, Zahn ordered a change of course and speed to throw off the German spotting. The *Walke* diary later

This is a view from inside the casemate of Turm 3 of Batterie Hamburg that was hit by a 5in. projectile on 24 June while engaging the destroyers USS *Walke* and *Forrest*. The projectile penetrated the front splinter shield and the subsequent detonation blew away the right-side splinter shield. Lt Nicholas Rudziak is seen sitting beside the gun, giving a good idea of its size. (Swan/Rudziak)

reported: 'It is fervently believed that this speed and course change enabled the writing of this report.' The second salvo narrowly missed *Walke*, striking slightly astern and off the starboard quarter about 15yd away, and dropping shrapnel on the deck.

In response to the German fire, both destroyers commenced emitting smoke. The minesweepers began retiring to the north using the cover of the smokescreen. The destroyers began to fire on Batterie Hamburg with 5in. AA-common rounds, the standard high-explosive type. From 1401 to 1419, Batterie Hamburg fired 19 salvoes against *Walke* without hitting it, but narrowly missing it on numerous occasions. The German fire was then shifted to the USS *Forrest*. At 1426, one round hit within 15m of the *Forrest*'s port bow and at 1427 another struck so close that a repair party was sent below deck for fear it might have caused underwater damage to the hull. The German fire was so accurate that the later after-action reports suggested that the Germans were using radar control. Batterie Hamburg ceased firing at 1428 as did the two destroyers which retired to Portland.

During the half-hour engagement, the destroyers fired 493 5in. rounds; 258 by the *Walke* and 235 by the *Forrest*. One 5in. projectile struck the splinter shield of Batterie Hamburg's Turm 3, killing three of the crew and wounding 11 men; this put the gun out of action. There were no casualties on any of the Allied ships.

OP PLAN #7-44

The mission for Bombardment Group 2 on 25 June consisted of three phases. Phase 1, starting at H-30 (1000) was to reduce two batteries of long-range German coastal guns. Phase 2 starting at 1120 was to neutralize two batteries of German medium-

The original target for the 25 June bombardment mission was 7./HKAA.1261, an army coastal gun battery located near Gatteville-le-Phare on the Pointe de Barfleur on the north-east corner of the Cotentin peninsula. This is one of its war-booty 155mm K420(f) field guns (St-Chamond Canon de 155 L Mod 16) still in its original kettle gun pit, enabling it to be used against advancing US Army forces to the south.

range field artillery guns. Phase 3 starting at 1300 was to provide fire support for VII Corps on request, with fire to be lifted no later than 1500.

Target selection was determined by the US Army's VII Corps, based on artillery fire directed against the advancing 4th Infantry Division over the previous days. Since the warships would be firing southward towards the US front lines, the targets were well to the east of the forward positions of the 22nd Infantry Regiment as of 24 June. Of the four principal targets, two were fortified coastal artillery batteries while the remainder were field batteries of Artillerie-Regiment.1709 of the 709.Infanterie-Division that had retreated to the coast during the previous few days of fighting. As can be seen, the intelligence depiction of the guns was somewhat mistaken. The field guns were generally under camouflage nets, so details were difficult to discern based on aerial photographs. The only major coastal artillery battery on the target list was HKB Gatteville located on the Pointe de Barfleur at the north-east tip of the Cotentin peninsula. The Schartenstand Programm had encased five of Gatteville's six powerful guns, limiting their fire out to sea. The one remaining 155mm K420(f)/St-Chamond Canon de 155 L Modèle (Mod) 16 was still located in its original kettle pit and had been firing at approaching US Army troops.

German Gun Batteries Targeted Under Op Plan #7-44		
Target	**Location**	**Notes**
Six 155mm guns in casemates	391275	Six 155mm K420(f); 7./HKAA.1261; MKB Gatteville
Four 150mm guns	304273	Four 76.2mm FK39(r); 9./AR.1709
Two 105mm guns	320291	Four 94mm Flak M39(e); MKB Blankenese
Four 105mm guns	205218	Four 155mm sFH 414 (f); 6./AR.1709

COMBAT

Bombardment Group 2 departed from the Portland area at 0330 in the pre-dawn of 25 June with the intention of making the most of the passage under cover of darkness. Adm Bryant used USS *Texas* as his flagship for the mission. The two battleships were the core of the force and were surrounded by an escort of destroyers. In the vanguard was Mine Squadron 7 directed by Cmdr Henry Plander, consisting of seven US Navy minesweepers, one Royal Navy minesweeper and four Royal Navy motor launches.

Visibility that morning was fair, with haze obscuring the shoreline at a range of 8,000 to 10,000yd. Smoke from fires in Cherbourg was carried out to sea by a light wind, sometimes masking the coast. The group arrived in Fire Support Area 2 about 0950 after the minesweepers had cleared the area. The intention was to begin bombarding the Gatteville battery at extreme range to complicate any spotting by German observers. This tactic was expected to reduce the accuracy of the German batteries. Spitfires from VCS-7 scouted the batteries and reported that there was no activity at Gatteville and that the site of the second battery south-east of Angoville seemed to be littered with dead Germans. Unknown to US planners, MKB Blankenese had been abandoned days before.

In the meantime, VII Corps commander Maj Gen Collins and First US Army commander Lt Gen Omar Bradley had reconsidered the navy fire support mission. The front lines reached by US Army forces were very fluid due to the collapse of German defences, and there was some concern that the naval gunfire would overshoot the targets and hit advancing VII Corps troops. The US Army forces in this sector were mainly from the 22nd Infantry Regiment, 4th Infantry Division. During the course of the day, the 2nd and 3rd Battalion of the 22nd Infantry reached the coast near Bretteville immediately east of Cherbourg. The US unit farthest east and closest to the planned bombardment was Company A, 70th Tank Battalion that was providing

An SFCP in action to the south-east of Cherbourg on 25 June 1944 during the naval bombardment. These joint Army/Navy teams coordinated the firing missions with US Navy ships offshore using the SCR-609 radio seen in this view.

tank support for the 22nd Infantry. This tank company was in the vicinity of the Maupertus air base, east of Bretteville and immediately south of Batterie Hamburg. Bradley and Collins decided to call off the planned fire support mission.

As a result of the Army decision, at 1000, the VII Corps headquarters instructed Adm Bryant to halt execution of Op. Plan 7-44 and to await fire requests from SFCPs ashore. *Texas* was assigned SFCP 36, the team with the 44th Field Artillery Battalion that was supporting the 22nd Infantry Regiment. Three other parties, SFCPs 33, 34 and 35, were also active, each attached to one of the battalions of the 22nd Infantry Regiment.

As a result of the change in plan, Mine Squadron 7 proceeded south-westward ahead of the main body to sweep Fire Support Areas 3 and 4 in case these areas were needed. The 22nd Infantry was operating closer to this area than to Fire Support Area 2, and so Bombardment Group 2 continued westward to facilitate any needed fire support. The destroyer *O'Brien* was ordered to accompany the minesweepers to provide smoke cover or to respond to any German actions. Bombardment Group 2 reached Fire Support Area 3 around noon.

The SFCP assigned to the USS *Arkansas* requested fire against Batterie Hamburg shortly after noon. Although Batterie Hamburg was not on the original list of targets, the bombardment group had an intelligence briefing that provided basic details of all

major German gun batteries in the vicinity of Cherbourg. Neither the records of the 22nd Infantry nor the USS *Arkansas* indicate what prompted this request, but it is likely that Batterie Hamburg had fired towards the advancing 22nd Infantry. Although the original plan had been to engage the German batteries at a range of about 18,000–20,000yd, by now the bombardment group was much closer to the coast, and only about 10,000yd from Batterie Hamburg.

A view of USS *Arkansas* under fire from Batterie Hamburg taken from the deck of USS *Texas* during the 25 June engagement.

A view of the stern of USS *Barton* (DD-722) from the deck of USS *Texas* on D-Day, 6 June 1944. *Barton* was the first US ship engaged by Batterie Hamburg on 25 June since it was escorting the minesweepers in the vanguard of the formation.

The *Arkansas* began firing its 12in. guns starting at 1208, expending 16 armour-piercing rounds over the course of about half an hour. The SFCP and the Spitfires overhead reported that there were two possible hits on Batterie Hamburg.

The German forward survey posts on Cap Lévy were slow reporting the approach of the warships due to the haze. *Texas* and *Arkansas* were jamming the German naval radars on Cap Lévy, making it difficult to get a precise bearing on the approaching warships. One German radar, believed to be a Würzburg fire control radar, was first detected by the US warships at 0930 but the signal was too weak to bother attempting to jam it. A second radar, probably a Seetakt naval surface-search radar, was picked up five minutes later due to its greater strength, but was continuously jammed through the morning and early afternoon. *Arkansas* also fired 14 3.5in. Window rockets which dispensed chaff to interfere with the radars.

Batterie Hamburg began firing around 1229 once the US Navy vessels had finally been spotted. The first three-gun salvo straddled the stern of the destroyer USS *Barton*

GUN DUEL OFF CHERBOURG, 25 JUNE 1944

Actions

1. At 0950, Bombardment Group 2 arrives in Fire Support Area 2.
2. US Army VII Corps HQ cancels original bombardment plans.
3. Mine Squadron 7 proceeds ahead to sweep Fire Support Areas 3 and 4.
4. At 1208, USS *Arkansas* begins firing its 12in. guns against Batterie Hamburg.
5. At 1229, Batterie Hamburg begins to engage Bombardment Group 2, straddling USS *Barton* and scoring one hit on the aft about one foot above the waterline but it fails to detonate.
6. At 1231, second salvo comes close to the bow of USS *Texas*. The third salvo at 1233 straddles the bow of the *Texas* and one round strikes *Laffey* but does not detonate.
7. The fourth salvo at 1235 straddles the stern of the *Texas*.
8. After 1235, *Texas* engages target at Grid 211230, the German battery 8./AR.1709.
9. By 1240, Bombardment Group 2 is shielded by smoke from the minesweepers and destroyers.
10. At 1240, USS *O'Brien* begins firing at Batterie Hamburg at a range of 13,700yd.
11. At 1245, *Texas* begins firing against Batterie Hamburg.
12. At 1248, Batterie Hamburg again targets *Texas*.
13. At 1250, Batterie Hamburg shifts its fire from the *Texas* to the destroyer *O'Brien*.
14. At 1251, the first salvo from Batterie Hamburg hits about 600yd over *O'Brien*, followed by a second salvo at 1252 that hits 300yd over. The third salvo around 1253 hits the bridge of *O'Brien*.
15. At 1255, Bombardment Group 2 is ordered to retire northward.
16. At 1255, the *Arkansas* begins firing against Target 19A based on spotting from the SFCP.
17. At 1304, *Texas* also engages Target 19A, the army field battery from 5./AR.1709.
18. At 1316, *Texas* is hit by Batterie Hamburg on the roof of the conning tower.
19. At 1320, the cruiser USS *Quincy* from Bombardment Group 1 off Cherbourg engages Batterie Hamburg.
20. Around 1330, Adm Bryant orders Bombardment Group 2 to navigate northward to a range of 18,000yd from Batterie Hamburg in the hopes of reducing the accuracy of the German fire. Around 1340, fire from Batterie Hamburg temporarily ceases.
21. At 1416, there is a three-round straddle of *Texas* from an unidentified German battery.
22. At 1444, Batterie Hamburg resumes firing.
23. At 1500, Bombardment Group 2 begins to retire back to Portland based on original schedule.

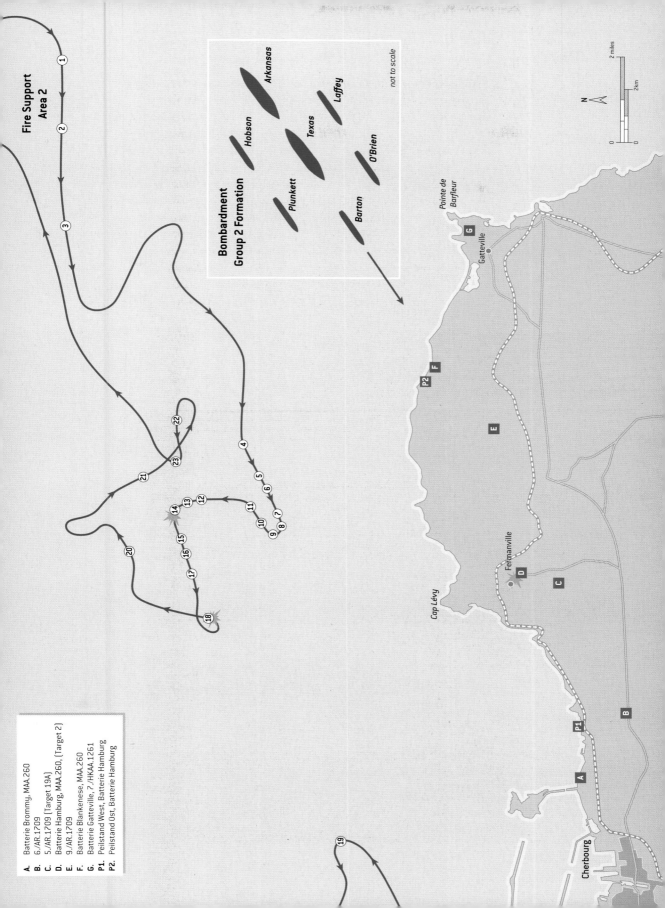

**Fire Support
Area 2**

**Bombardment
Group 2 Formation**

Hobson

Arkansas

Plunkett

Texas

Laffey

Barton

O'Brien

not to scale

N

2 miles

2km

0

*Pointe de
Barfleur*

G

Gatteville

F

P2

E

Cap Lévy

Fermanville

D

C

P1

A

B

Cherbourg

1
2
3
4
5
6
7
8
9
10
11
12
13
14
15
16
17
18
19
20
21
22
23

A. Batterie Brommy, MAA.260
B. 6./AR.1709
C. 5./AR.1709 [Target 19A]
D. Batterie Hamburg, MAA.260, [Target 2]
E. 9./AR.1709
F. Batterie Blankenese, MAA.260
G. Batterie Gatteville, 7./HKAA.1261
P1. Peilstand West, Batterie Hamburg
P2. Peilstand Ost, Batterie Hamburg

and scored one hit on the aft about one foot above the waterline. The projectile failed to detonate. Of the five hits scored by Batterie Hamburg during the course of the day, three failed to detonate. Some of the projectiles did not impact the ship directly, but ricocheted off the water and then struck the ships, damaging the impact fuse in the process. It is also possible that the old ammunition had faulty fuses.

The second salvo from Batterie Hamburg at 1231 came close to the bow of *Texas* and another projectile impact completely enveloped one of the minesweepers with spray over its port bow. A subsequent impact was about 200yd in front of *Texas*; a US Navy after-action report suggested that the miss was due to the incorrect estimate of the German plotting room in assessing the speed of the *Texas*. The third salvo at 1233 straddled the bow of *Texas*. A projectile impacted near the port bow of the destroyer *Laffey* and ricocheted into the ship under the anchor causing a gash one foot high and four feet long but it did not detonate. The fourth salvo at 1235 straddled the stern of *Texas* and was described as 'very close'.

GERMAN ENGAGEMENT PRACTICES

A projectile from Batterie Hamburg impacts behind USS *Texas* during the 25 June engagement as viewed from USS *Arkansas*.

There are no detailed records from Batterie Hamburg of the engagement with Bombardment Group 2 on 25 June. However, it is possible to recreate the likely sequence of the engagement based on German Navy manuals.

The battery commander began the sequence by announcing via the telephone: 'Enemy warship approaching from the right. Lay on – right funnel, left edge. Observe!' This command instructed the two survey posts to begin feeding data to the plotting room, with the left edge of the ship's funnel as the aiming point. The inclination officer then reported 'Bow left. Inclination minus 3. Speed 10 knots'. The two remote survey posts had been alerted and began passing on their data: 'Black (eastern survey post) 6380'; 'Red (western survey post) 0775'. The survey posts continued to pass along the data since it changed as the ship moved. In a monotonous sequence, the right survey post reported '6382; 6384; 6385'. As this data was received in the plotting room, the data was inputted into the Long-Base Device in the plotting room of the Leitstand. The range-reader followed the calculations of the device and reported to the plotting officer: 'Range 10,300'. The bearing-reader likewise reported 'Bearing 0370 mils'. The plotting officer passed this on to the battery commander and meteorological team: 'First bearing 0370, first range 10,300'. The meteorological team then calculated for wind-drift and reported 'Meteor for wind bearing 02, range 11,000'.

This process was non-stop since the ship continued to move, sometimes in an evasive fashion. So the range- and bearing-readers continued to report new data based on the output from the Long-Base Device which was periodically corrected by the plotting officer based on input from the survey posts. Once the battery commander was confident that they had established the basic trajectory data, it was passed to the gun crew from the plotting room via telephone.

The firing sequence began when the battery commander gave the gun crew final ammunition instructions 'Charge-normal. Fuse-instantaneous. Shell armour piercing. All guns ranging. Fire by order of the plotting officer. From the right – Fire!' These instructions told the gun crew the amount of propellant, type of ammunition and the fuse to use. The first salvo was generally considered a 'ranging' salvo since it was presumed it would miss. Generally, the technique was to use 'laddering' with the first salvo expected to land on the other side of the ship. This was better than having it

USS *Texas* manoeuvring to avoid fire from Batterie Hamburg on 25 June with impacts visible in the water. A layer of smoke can be seen on the horizon to the right where accompanying minesweepers and destroyers were attempting to shield the bombardment group. This photo was taken from one of the accompanying destroyers.

impact on the near-side of the ship since the splash would obscure the target. When the first salvo landed, the battery would 'climb down the ladder' bringing each successive salvo closer to the target.

When the first salvo was fired, the various plotting crews began their stopwatches on the sound of the guns firing, and halted the stopwatch based on reports of impacts from the survey posts. At a range of 15,000m, it could take 40 to 50 seconds for the rounds to fly out to the target. The process began again with necessary corrections based on the location of the miss, as well as continual reporting on the movement of the target ship. Once the impacts began to straddle the target ship, the battery commander would order 'Five rounds. From the right. Rapid Fire!' Corrections would have continued to be put into the Long-Base Device until the target was hit.

The first salvoes from Batterie Hamburg landed about 45 seconds apart, an extremely fast reload time for this type of gun and indicative of a well-trained and well-rested crew. *Texas* and *Arkansas* were the primary targets of Batterie Hamburg's initial salvoes, no doubt due to their greater visibility in the hazy conditions. The *Texas* after-action report recalled:

> Shell after shell landed close, one near miss abreast the bridge throwing sheets of water over the bridge and superstructure. Fragments rained down on the topsides, Flag Bridge, and Secondary Forward. Fortunately, all AA [anti-aircraft] personnel were under cover on the starboard (unengaged) side and no casualties resulted although personnel on the 5in. battery in the port air-castle had some near missies. This shell was so close that Spot Two reported he could not see where it hit in the water because of the freeboard. It was believed at the time that this was a hit at the waterline and Central Station was ordered to investigate. But it was soon reported there was no damage other than a considerable loss of paint.

The USS *O'Brien* (DD-725) suffered the most damage of any of the ships in Bombardment Group 2 with a direct hit on its bridge. This is a view of the ship after repairs in 1945.

During one of the salvoes, a 240mm projectile ricocheted off the water near *Texas* and penetrated into the officers' quarters near Frame 19-Port on the half-deck, but failed to explode. The space was not occupied and the penetration was not discovered until later in the afternoon. The salvoes from Batterie Hamburg usually consisted of three 240mm projectiles, sometimes accompanied by a few smaller rounds from the battery's secondary 75mm guns.

At 1235, a VCS-7 Spitfire reported that firing was observed from Grid 211230. This was the location of 8./AR.1709, but it is unlikely that this army battery would have been able to engage *Texas*. More likely the pilot saw the flash of guns that were actually directed at US Army troops east of Cherbourg. Alternately, the pilot may have misreported fire from Batterie Brommy that was located farther west. In the event, *Texas*

The most serious damage to USS *Texas* occurred when a projectile from Batterie Hamburg struck the roof of the armoured conning tower in the lower right, skidded over the roof and detonated against the support arm below the pilothouse above.

fired only once at this target. An after-action report noted: 'Spotting was very erratic and confusing. In many cases, the SFCP and plane gave spots in the opposite directions. It is believed that this was caused by the fact that several ships were firing simultaneously at targets in close proximity to each other, and consequently spotters were unable to identify the fall of shot.'

By 1240, Bombardment Group 2 was shielded by smokescreens from the minesweepers and destroyers. The *Arkansas* war diary noted: 'The German fire was very accurate and had it not been for the very excellent smoke screens put up by the mine-sweepers and destroyers, the commanding officer feels more damage would have been done to our heavy ships.' From the difficulties that Batterie Hamburg had in targeting the group in the presence of smoke, it became evident that the battery was relying on rangefinders and other optical devices and not radar for fire control.

USS *Texas* began firing against Batterie Hamburg at 1245 on 25 June. The American gun flashes could be seen through the smoke by Batterie Hamburg's forward survey posts and so German fire resumed at 1248, falling close to starboard and aft of *Texas*. At 1304, *Texas* scored an 'own goal' when the right gun of Turret 2 swivelled and struck the right gun of Turret 1, putting it out of action for the time being. Bryant decided to move the bombardment group northward, away from Batterie Hamburg, to make it more difficult for the Germans to aim at the warships.

The destroyer *O'Brien* began firing at Batterie Hamburg at 1240 at a range of 13,700yd. It walked the fire into the target in 100yd increments using the usual ladder method until impacting the battery area. Several rounds fell around Batterie Hamburg's casemates and some may have impacted the bunkers. However, the 5in.

projectiles were too weak to penetrate the thick concrete. In response, Batterie Hamburg shifted its fire from *Texas* to *O'Brien* around 1250. The first salvo from Batterie Hamburg at 1251 hit about 600yd over the *O'Brien*, followed by a second salvo at 1252 that hit 300yd over. The third salvo straddled *O'Brien*, with a single projectile impacting the aft upper starboard corner of the bridge, knocking out all the ship's radar and putting the CIC out of operation. This explosion also wrecked the forward twin 40mm gun mount. Three men on the bridge, one in the CIC, and all nine men on the 40mm gun tub were killed instantly and a further two officers and 17 men were wounded. The *O'Brien* continued to fire for another two minutes but then ceased firing at 1255 when Bombardment Group 2 began retiring northward. The deck log of *O'Brien* later recalled

> Damage to the enemy was not observed because of the haze and difficulty determining effects of gunfire on the heavily casemated battery. The shore battery was still firing when this group retired. However, it is believed that fire from this vessel must have had some effect in order to cause the shore battery to shift fire from the heavy ships to the USS *O'Brien*.

At 1255, *Arkansas* began firing against 'Target 19A' based on spotting from the SFCP. *Texas* followed suit at 1304. This was probably an army field battery, 5./AR.1709. At 1320, the cruiser USS *Quincy* from Bombardment Group 1 off Cherbourg harbour was instructed by its SFCP to engage Batterie Hamburg, but the air spotting was so confusing that 'very little effective fire was delivered on it'.

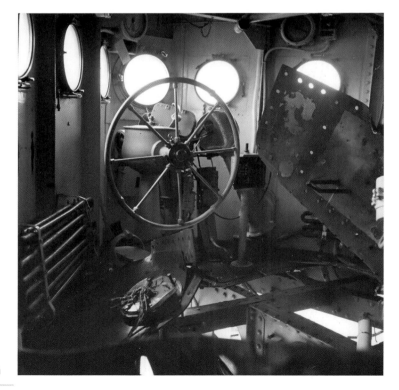

A view of the forward portion of the pilothouse of USS *Texas* showing the damage caused by the explosion of the 240mm projectile on the conning tower below. The blast buckled several of the floor plates, severely injuring the navigation crew.

Texas suffered its most serious damage at 1316 when a high-explosive projectile from Batterie Hamburg struck the roof of the conning tower, skidded across the armoured top plate, and detonated against the supporting column of the pilothouse. The projectile initially sheared off the periscope of the Mark 21 Director No. 3 on the roof of the conning tower, collapsing the director housing on to the Gunnery Officer, Lt Cmdr Richard Derickson, severely injuring him and three other men. The detonation of the projectile had devastating effects above the conning tower, smashing underneath the Navigation Bridge and Ship Control Party. All personnel in the forward part of the bridge were severely injured since the blast blew the decking upward about four feet, causing compound fractures of the men's legs. The helmsman was killed

The executive officer of USS *Texas*, Commander Jose Cabanillas, examines the damage to the navigation bridge after the battleship returned to Portsmouth.

and six other men were severely injured. Navigation was taken over by the conning tower and fire control was taken over by the plotting room.

In the midst of this turmoil, *Texas* continued to be straddled while its 14in. guns continued their fire against Batterie Hamburg. In the chaos, a fire was started on the fantail when the blast from the 14in. gun turret directly aft set the canvas covers over the 40mm ammunition lockers on fire, and blew 40mm ammunition clips out of their ready racks on to the deck. The 14in. guns usually fired broadside, not directly over the fantail. The ship's Marine detachment began tossing the loose 40mm ammunition over the sides to prevent accidental detonations and put out the assorted fires.

Adm Bryant ordered Bombardment Group 2 to continue northward to a range of 18,000yd from Batterie Hamburg. Around 1340, fire from Batterie Hamburg temporarily ceased as the German spotters lost sight of their targets in the midday haze. *Texas* and *Arkansas* continued firing at the German battery as they sailed northward. At 1416, there was a three-round straddle from an unidentified German battery, probably Batterie Brommy. Batterie Hamburg resumed firing at 1444 and *Texas* recorded 'many splashes close aboard'.

The original plan had been to conduct the fire support mission until 1500. With the cut-off time approaching, Bryant contacted the US Army VII Corps headquarters. By the afternoon of 25 June, the German defences in Cherbourg were collapsing and there was no further need for naval fire support. VII Corps reaffirmed the cut-off time of 1500 and, as a result, Bombardment Group 2 broke off the inconclusive engagement and headed back to Portland.

ANALYSIS

Bombardment Group 2 believed it had scored some hits on Batterie Hamburg, but none of the three remaining 240mm guns had been knocked out. Batterie Hamburg later reported to headquarters in Cherbourg that they had sunk one cruiser and damaged another, later claiming that the second had sunk. In fact, only two ships, *Texas* and *O'Brien*, had suffered any significant damage.

The report by Vice Admiral C.F. Bryant after the Cherbourg action provides a concise assessment of the day's actions:

> A major caliber, heavily casemated, or turreted, and well-dispersed coast defense battery cannot be silenced by bombardment without excess expenditure of ammunition and great risk to the bombarding force unless the firing can be carried out from a blind bearing or from a greater range than that of the shore battery. The original plans for the bombardment of Cherbourg provided for bombardment of major caliber batteries from the maximum effective range of the ships available, but this phase of the operation was cancelled at the last minute. Even had it not been cancelled it is doubtful that all of the guns could have been destroyed due to the small probability of making direct hits on the small target area presented by one gun turret or casemated emplacements. Such a mission should not be undertaken unless its successful accomplishment is of sufficient importance to justify unrestricted expenditures of ammunition and the risk of serious damage to the bombarding force.
>
> In a sense, the mission assigned this task group was accomplished in that all calls for fire support made by the army through the SFCPs were delivered. However, it is doubtful that the damage inflicted on the enemy materially assisted the army in its advance on Cherbourg. No calls for fire were received by the *Texas* and only three were received by the *Arkansas*, one of which was for fire on Target #2 [Batterie Hamburg], the battery of

major caliber guns which menaced the entire bombardment force and was still in action upon retirement. It is very unlikely that this battery menaced the army approach from inland.

Batterie Hamburg's fire against the naval group was persistent and determined. The *Texas* war diary later noted: 'That there could have been so many straddles and near misses with so few hits and consequent little damage is most amazing and lucky. One member of Repair IV counted sixty-five solid explosions and a probably thirty straddles. Unfortunately, the Chief Recorder in the bridge was one of the badly wounded and his records ended with the hit.'

US Navy Ammunition Expenditure on 25 June 1944			
Ship	14-inch	12-inch	5-inch
Texas	110 HC, 94 AP		
Arkansas		58 AP	
Barton			99
O'Brien			192
Laffey			121
Hobson			73
Plunkett			67
Total	**204**	**58**	**552**

There are no detailed German records of damage to Batterie Hamburg for 25 June, though it is possible that some of the bunkers or secondary guns were hit. Although Spitfire spotting aircraft repeatedly reported hits on the battery site, nothing short of a direct hit on the guns would have disabled them. A hit on the casemate itself near the gun might have killed or injured some of the gun crew, but was unlikely to have disabled a gun. The failure to hit any of the guns was not a surprise to the US Navy ships based on earlier engagements against coastal batteries in 1943–44.

To put this accuracy issue into some perspective, it is worth examining other examples where ballistic data is available. For example, there is a considerable amount of data on the performance of the German 88mm Flak gun used in an anti-tank role in 1941–42. This provides an almost ideal example of the use of a high-performance gun against small targets since the gun was mounted on a very stable cruciform platform and aimed in a direct-fire mode using a powerful telescopic sight. At typical combat ranges of 2.5–3km, these guns usually required 10–15 rounds to hit an enemy tank. At longer ranges, ammunition expenditure went up to over 20 rounds per tank. This was the best-case scenario for a gun firing on a target as small as the gun embrasure of Batterie Hamburg.

Gun accuracy is heavily dependent on range. In the case of the US Army's 155mm M1917 coastal gun, it required 5.5 rounds on average to hit a small target (1 square yard) at 3,000yd, 24 rounds at 5,000yd, 315 rounds at 10,000yd, 665 rounds at 12,500yd and 2,500 rounds at 15,000yd. The gun embrasure of Batterie Hamburg was about 2–3 square yards in size. In other words, the chances of hitting a small target such as the Batterie Hamburg embrasure was very unlikely at ranges over 10,000yd such as during the 25 June engagement, even for a stationary gun.

Naval guns are at a serious disadvantage compared to land-based artillery since the ship is a moving platform and even small movements drastically decrease gun accuracy. On 25 June, USS *Texas* was violently manoeuvring during much of the engagement, making direct hits on Batterie Hamburg even less likely.

The ineffectiveness of USS *Texas* and other ships against Batterie Hamburg was also due to the design of the gun casemates. Earlier studies of ship-vs-gun battery engagements such as Pantelleria found that ships were unlikely to hit coastal guns but were able to neutralize the batteries by disrupting the communications between their fire control bunkers and interrupting their supply of ammunition between the ammunition bunkers and the guns. In the case of Batterie Hamburg, neither of these factors played a role. Batterie Hamburg was never subjected to heavy bomber attack, and as a result, the buried cables between the fire control bunker and the gun casemates were not disrupted. Although it was possible that some cables were ripped up by naval gunfire during the 25 June gun duel, it was extremely unlikely. German gun batteries typically used armoured cable buried 2m or more below the surface that was not especially vulnerable to naval gunfire short of a direct impact. The large casemates used by Batterie Hamburg also limited the disruption of the ammunition supply since they contained an exceptionally large ammunition reserve.

In contrast, Batterie Hamburg fired 96 to 98 rounds from each of its three functional 240mm guns for a total of about 290 rounds and scored five hits. Only two

The Turm 1 gun of Batterie Hamburg in early July 1944 being inspected by a First US Army survey team. Lt Nicholas Rudziak is seen holding one of the gun's brass propellant casings. Several of the guns had objects in their barrels, remnants of attempts by the German crews to spike them before the battery's surrender. (Swan/Rudziak)

of these were direct hits while three others were near misses that ricocheted off the water into the ships. Batterie Hamburg had numerous advantages over the opposing warships since its guns were firing from stable platforms, and its targets, though moving, were large targets. Even if Batterie Hamburg managed a few hits during the 25 June gun duel, it was ultimately ineffective.

A post-war US Navy study of amphibious operations concluded:

> The coastal defence gun turned out to be a 'paper tiger', in spite of the enormous resources that the Germans and Japanese devoted to that system [in World War II]. Coastal defense guns never succeeded in interfering significantly with transport unloadings or with landing craft and control vessels engaged in the ship-to-shore movement. Occasionally, a transport had to shift its unloading position or a 'small boy' engaged in close-in minesweeping was hit, but very few surface combatants or amphibious ships were even damaged; none were sunk.

The Seeko Kanalküste (Sea Commander, Channel Coast) later claimed that Kriegsmarine batteries in France sank three heavy cruisers, one light cruiser, one transport ship and various smaller vessels; army coastal batteries were credited with a destroyer and some other vessels. These claims were mainly based on Batterie Hamburg's claims and the Crisbecq battery's claim of the USS *Corry*. With the possible exception of the USS *Corry*, Atlantikwall coastal guns never sank a significant Allied warship in 1943–45. Only one large non-combatant was sunk, the Liberty ship SS *Sambut*. German gun batteries did sink many landing craft during the Normandy landings and during subsequent battles such as Walcheren island. During Operation *Neptune*, the Allies lost nearly 300 landing craft of various types; however, much of this damage was caused by the obstacle belts including mines and obstructions. Those lost to gunfire were mainly hit near the shoreline by direct-fire weapons such as 50mm pedestal guns as well as field guns and anti-tank guns in the 75mm to 88mm range, and not by large-calibre coastal guns.

The main effect of the Atlantikwall fortification programme was to discourage Allied planners from selecting well-defended ports as the objective of major amphibious operations in favour of weakly defended, open coastline. The weaker concentrations of coastal guns such as those facing the *Neptune* and *Dragoon* landings failed to significantly interfere with the amphibious landings.

Although not addressed here directly, the most critical advantage of naval gunfire during amphibious operations in the Mediterranean and in North-West Europe in 1942–44 was the ability to protect the beachhead against German counter-attacks. Naval gunfire was instrumental in defending the beachheads at Sicily and Salerno in 1943, and again at Anzio and Normandy in 1944, against German Panzer counter-attacks.

AFTERMATH

Batterie Hamburg remained isolated in the days following the 25 June gun duel. The number of troops within the strongpoint swelled with troops from neighbouring batteries that had been overrun by the US Army advance.

The German commander of Festung Cherbourg, Gen Maj Karl von Schlieben, surrendered on 26 June. He claimed that he could not order the German garrisons elsewhere on the northern side of the Cotentin peninsula to follow his instructions. The US VII Corps ordered the 4th Infantry Division to clean up remaining German pockets of resistance east of Cherbourg on 26 June.

Sherman tanks of Company A, 70th Tank Battalion approached Batterie Hamburg on 26 June and began firing, but the Germans responded using some of the anti-tank guns they had acquired from Saint-Pierre-Église a few days before. Waving a flag of truce, a delegation from the 22nd Infantry Regiment approached Batterie Hamburg and demanded its surrender. Stalling for time, Gelbhaar responded that it was not his decision to make, but that of his commanding officer. Major Friedrich Küppers was the leader of Artillerie-Gruppe Montebourg and was holed up in the nearby cluster of fortifications called Panzerwerk Osteck (Stützpunkt 235).

On 27 June, a delegation from the 4th Infantry Division arrived outside Osteck and demanded its surrender. After three hours of negotiations, Küppers signed a capitulation order late that day that obligated all troops under his command to surrender, including Gelbhaar and his battery. On the morning of 28 June, the battery began destroying its guns and emplacements using explosive charges. In response, the neighbouring US troops warned that any further demolitions would be answered by artillery fire. As a result, further destruction of equipment used less noisy techniques, with all the 240mm guns spiked. The surrender of Batterie Hamburg finally took place at 1300 on 28 June.

In late June, USS *Texas* replenished ammunition and fuel in England. In early August, it sailed for southern France, taking part in the bombardment of the Südwall as part of the 15 August Operation *Dragoon* landings. In early 1945, *Texas* returned to the Pacific where it took part in the bombardments of Iwo Jima and Okinawa.

The guns of Batterie Hamburg were scrapped after the war, and the site returned to its original French owners. Today, the ruins are heavily overgrown and are on private property not accessible to the public. In 1947, USS *Texas* was turned over to the state of Texas to serve as a museum ship near San Jacinto. It was the first and oldest of the eight US battleships that became permanent floating museums. When this book was written in 2022, the ship was temporarily closed to visitors in preparation for the transfer to a dry dock for another major overhaul to deal with hull leaks.

A frontal view of USS *Texas* taken in 2018. (CC BY-SA 4.0; Gronowski26 via Wikimedia Commons)

BIBLIOGRAPHY

This book was based primarily on archival sources. Accounts of the US Navy ships were based on the logs and reports located in Record Group 38 at the US National Archives and Records Administration in College Park, Maryland. The sections dealing with the Atlantikwall were based on various German documents including the Kriegmarine's *Lagemeldungen Küstenverteidigung* and the war diary of the OKM (Oberkommando der Kriegsmarine). There are numerous accounts on the Atlantikwall in the US Army's Foreign Military Studies series. Due to space reasons, they are not listed here but can be found in the author's three books on the Atlantikwall in the Osprey Fortress series.

BOOKS

Chazette, Alain, *Mur de l'Atlantique: Les batteries de côte en Normandie de Havre à Cherbourg*, Histoire et Fortifications, Vertou: 2011

Doyle, David, *USS Texas*, Squadron Signal, Carrollton: 2012

Ferguson, Jon, *Historic Battleship Texas: The Last Dreadnought*, State House Press, Abilene: 2007

Forrest, Michael, *The Defence of the Dardanelles: From Bombards to Battleships*, Pen & Sword, Barnsley: 2012

Friedman, Norman, *Naval Firepower: Battleship Guns and Gunnery in the Dreadnought Era*, Naval Institute, Annapolis: 2008

Friedman, Norman, *Naval Weapons of World War One*, Seaforth, Barnsley: 2011.

Karau, Mark, *The Naval Flank of the Western Front: The German Marine-Korps Flandern 1914–1918*, Seaforth, Barnsley: 2014

Morison, Samuel E., *History of US Naval Operations in WWII: The Invasion of France and Germany 1944–1945*, Little, Brown, New York: 1957

Rahn, Werner and Gerhard Schreiber, *Kriegstagebuch der Seekriegsleitung 1939–1945*, Teil A, Band 58/1 1. bis 15. Juni 1944; Band 58/II 16. bis 30. Juni 1944, E.S. Mittler & Sohn, Berlin: 1995

Rolf, Rudi, *Der Atlantikwall: Die Bauten der deutschen Küstenbefestigungen 1940–45*, Zeller, Osnabrück: 1998

Sakkers, Hans and Marc Machielse, *Artillerieduell der Fernkampfgeschütze am Pas de Calais 1940–1944*, Helios, Aachen: 2013

Schmeelke, Michael, *Artillerie an der Küste: Die Deutsche Marine, das Heer und die Luftwaffe in der Küstenverteidigung 1939–1945*, VDM, Zweibrücken: 2021

Wiper, Steve and Tom Flowers, *USS Texas BB-35*, Classic Warship Publishing, Tucson: 2006

Zaloga, Steven J., *The Atlantic Wall (1): France*, Osprey Publishing Ltd, Oxford: 2007

Zaloga, Steven J., *The Atlantic Wall (2): Belgium, The Netherlands, Denmark and Norway*, Osprey Publishing Ltd, Oxford: 2009

Zaloga, Steven J., *The Atlantic Wall (3): The Sudwall*, Osprey Publishing Ltd, Oxford: 2015

ARTICLES

Benbow, Tim, 'Battleships, D-Day, and Naval Strategy', *War in History*, June 2021, n.p.

Schmalenbach, Paul, 'German Navy Large Bore Guns Operational Ashore during World War I', *Warship International*, Vol. 20. No. 2, (1983) pp. 131–148

Sims, Philip, 'German Coast Artillery in Belgium in World War I', *Coast Defense Study Group Journal*, November 1998, pp. 119–125

US Army troops march German prisoners of war through Cherbourg on 28 June 1944, after the city's liberation.

INDEX